NATIONAL CATHOLIC EDUCATIONAL ASSOCIATION

THE POWER OF OUR IDEAS

Papers from the 1992 Principals Academy

Co-directors:
Regina Haney, OSF
Director of Curriculum/NCEA

Dr. Robert Kealey
Executive Director of Elementary Schools/NCEA

Editors:
Patricia Feistritzer
Director of Communications/NCEA

Anne Walsh, RSHM
Faculty in Residence
Fordham University

Copyright 1993
National Catholic Educational Association
1077 30th Street, NW • Suite 100 • Washington, DC 20007-3852 • (202) 337-6232
ISBN 1-55833-096-8

Design by Tia Gray, cover design and photos by Beatriz Ruiz

National Catholic Principals Academy
July 1992

Row 1 (left to right): Dr. Robert Kealey, Richard Martinez, Barbara O'Block, Michael A. Casper, Ruth M. Frere, Sr. Regina Haney, John J. Burke, James T. Brennan.

Row 2: George Hofbauer, Sr. Joseph Spring, Sr. Francis Christi Beck, Donna Marie O'Brien, Sr. Carol Seidl, Sr. Julia Dias Fonseca, Helen S. Smith, Sr. Catherine Kamphaus, Becky Piela.

Row 3: Carol Speltz, Sr. Mary Byrnes, Cheri Gardner, Ellen C. Herron, Sr. Lorraine Burns, Sr. Ann Christi Brink, Barbara Mathe, Barbara K. McClure, Paul E. DeZarn.

Row 4: Sr. Dawn Gear, Sr. Aidan Hogan, Kathleen M. Adams, Paula DeKeersgieter, Carmen E. Heflin, Linda L. Cherry, Sr. Joel Miller, Sr. Valerie Grondin.

Table of Contents

Introduction

From the Capitol inaugural stand on January 20, 1993, President Clinton invoked all Americans to do their part to renew our country, to revitalize our democracy. What method or medium did he suggest for the accomplishment of this challenge? President Clinton reminded us that, "our greatest strength is the power of our ideas, which are still new."

During the summer of 1992, thirty-two elementary Catholic school administrators—gathered in Washington, DC, to participate in the 1992 Principals Academy—had the opportunity to foreshadow the power of which Clinton spoke. Thus the title of this volume of Papers from the Principals Academy, *The Power Of Our Ideas.*

Principals selected from Catholic schools nationwide experienced both personal revitalization and a renewed hope in the durability of Catholic schools during the academy. The power of their ideas was strengthened through sharing and networking with one another, learning more about the research and beliefs of leaders in the field of Catholic education, and writing this handbook.

The topics addressed here relate to the issues focused on during the academy. These are Leadership, Public Policy, School and Society, and Educational Technology. These issues are taken from the priority directional statements that evolved through the National Congress on Catholic Schools for the 21st Century (see page viii).

Like President Clinton, we at NCEA believe that America will be better because of the powerhouse of ideas that we can generate together. It is our special hope that this book will spark fresh conviction and commitment from other principals, thus ensuring the future of our Catholic schools.

Special thanks to Pat Feistritzer and Sister Anne Walsh for editing, and to Beatriz Ruiz and Tia Gray for the design.

Dr. Robert Kealey
Regina Haney, OSF

National Congress on Catholic Schools for the 21st Century

Priority Directional Statements

We will challenge the entire Catholic community and others to make a radical commitment to Catholic schools and generous investment in them.

We will guarantee opportunities for ongoing spiritual formation for Catholic school faculties, staff and leadership.

We will challenge the U.S. bishops to implement the November 1990 statement on Catholic schools, since their leadership is critical to the future of Catholic schools.

We will aggressively pursue legislation enabling parents to choose the education appropriate for their children with their share of the education tax dollar.

We will organize broad-based coalitions to lobby on every level in order to achieve equal educational opportunities for all children, parents and educators.

We will educate students to meet the intellectual, social and ethical challenges of living in a technological and global society.

We will actively identify, select and develop Catholic school leaders who espouse gospel values and demonstrate professional competencies.

We will establish governance structures which give all those committed to the Catholic school's mission the power and responsibility to achieve it.

Section I
Leadership

Initiating a Catholic School Board: A Timeline

Rationale

Since the beginning of Catholic schools, there has been a need for a form of educational governance. After Vatican Council II, the call went out for each parish to initiate a finance committee, a parish council and a school board.

In the 1972 document *To Teach As Jesus Did,* an even clearer mandate was issued as follows:

> On the diocesan level, the educational mission can best be coordinated by a single board of education concerned with the needs of the entire local church. Many such boards have already been established and are now rendering important service to the church and education. They work best when they are broadly representative of all the people of the diocese, laity, priests and religious. Membership would be open to people of many points of view, including those who may perceive needs and advocate approaches different from those expressed in this pastoral. (141)

In 1983, the Code of Canon Law required consultative groups in each diocese and parish (cc. 492, 495, 502, 537).

In November of 1991, the National Catholic Educational Association held the National Congress of Catholic Schools for the 21st Century. As part of this Congress, belief and directional statements were written to enable the growth of boards.

To assist in initiating a school board, this paper will develop a practical timeline. Individual principals will need to examine the local situation and set goals for a workable timeline for their specific school. The following outline is a suggested format within which to accomplish this need.

September. Set meeting with pastor to discuss the initiation of a

3

school board, presenting positive reasons for its need at this time. The board will be an additional support to the pastor and principal in the difficult areas of policy development, decision making and financial needs For example, the board could be responsible for creating a five-year income plan with realistic goals in the areas of tuition and subsidies. It will also prove to be a challenging new way of accomplishing the church's educational ministry.

A second, follow-up meeting takes place to confirm the support of the pastor in initiating a board. With the affirmation of pastor and principal, a selection of a five-member task force is made. These members are personally contacted and invited to meet with the pastor and principal to discuss the future school board.

October. The task force meets to set goals for the development of the school board for the following September. The *Building Better Boards* video program, produced and developed by the NCEA, is used to educate the group. This program includes information about the significance and basic concepts of boards, as well as their roles and responsibilities.

November. The task force, pastor and principal discuss the type of board needed for the school, with consideration given to diocesan guidelines and specific school needs. They divide themselves into two committees.

One group works on developing a constitution. This project is scheduled for completion by the February meeting. Samples of constitutions can be found in the Appendix of *Building Better Boards.*

The second group is designated a selection committee. They are responsible for recruiting possible candidates for the board. This selection is to be completed by March. (See the sample application on page 6.)

Candidates from the following varied groups might be considered: alumni, parents, parishioners, former teachers, community leaders and neighboring business owners. Committee members refer to the *Building Better Boards* handbook from NCEA to establish eligibility requirements and qualifications for use in their selection of candidates.

December. The task force continues working on assigned committees and meets to report on progress to date. The discussion includes the relationship of this new school board to the other groups in the parish, i.e., the parish council and the home-school association. At the December faculty meeting, the principal and pastor share information regarding the formation of a school board, using the *Building Better Boards* video. The philosophy of the school is incorporated into this discussion.

January. During the regular January parents' meeting, the principal and pastor give a report on the development of the school board. The rationale and purpose of this board are shared and the task force members are introduced. Discussion and questions are entertained for further clarification. Applications are available to parents and the necessary qualifications for eligibility are explained to those who are interested in board membership.

February. The principal, pastor and task force meet to continue the development of the constitution. Applications for board membership are reviewed and discussed.

March. The nine newly selected members meet and an in-service program is provided. The *Building Better Boards* video program is used.

The members of the board, the pastor and principal determine the specific organizational roles that each assumes. The principal submits a written report quarterly; the pastor submits an annual financial report; and the chairperson, with the assistance of the executive board, prepares an agenda 10 days before each monthly meeting. In order for this process to be of assistance to the school community, all must be eager to participate in these tasks.

April. Continued in-service is given. Members have an opportunity to discuss church documents, and to formulate a school philosophy and policies, as well as to consider funding sources.

The board members select a chairperson, in the context of prayer and discernment. The term of service for each member is determined.

May. Following a Saturday afternoon of recollection, the new school board is installed at the Sunday liturgy. A reception is held after the liturgy to introduce the board members to the parishioners.

June. The executive committee of the school board meets to set the agenda and meeting dates for the next school year.

Resources

Building Better Boards Handbook and Video Program, Washington, DC, NCEA, 1990, 1991.

Canon Law Society of America, *The Code of Canon Law,* Washington, DC, Canon Law Society of America, 1983.

Catholic Schools for the 21st Century: Executive Summary, Washington, DC, NCEA, 1991.

National Conference of Catholic Bishops, *To Teach As Jesus Did,* U.S. Catholic Conference, Washington, DC, 1972.

Sample Application for a School Board Member

Name _____

Address _____

Apt. No._____Zip Code _____

    Phone Nos.
    Home _____

Work_____

Educational Background
    High School _____

    College _____

    Other _____

Present Occupation _____

No. of Years in Parish _____

Reasons for wanting to be a school board member

_____

_____

_____

_____

Francis Christi Beck, SSJ
Our Lady of Confidence School
Philadelphia, Pennsylvania

Mary Byrnes, PBVM
St. Catherine of Genoa School
New York, New York

The Time Has Come to Blow Our Horn!

The dust has begun to settle from the National Congress of Catholic Schools, whose purpose was to revitalize plans for the future of Catholic schooling. Now principals are becoming aware of the substantive groundwork that has been laid to formulate a vision and chart a course for our schools in the 21st century. Directional statements and strategies formulated at the national level are designed to inspire principals, parents and board members at the grass-roots level. If we believe in Catholic schools, Robert Kealey says, we must "tell the world of their magic and tell it with tongues of fire."

Catholic schools work

Research has confirmed what we already know: Catholic schools work. Several studies have shown that Catholic school students excel in reading, science and mathematical performance. A strong sense of community continues to be a distinctive quality of Catholic education. Coleman's study indicates that this sense of community support and involvement greatly influences the strong academic performance of students.

In regard to values, NCEA research reveals that Catholic school students tend to support marriage and family values, community involvement and service for others. These values contribute to a greatly improved society.

We know that, given the same dollar, we use it more effectively than our public school counterparts. Catholic schools have shown themselves to be models of efficiency. As we examine our schools in the light of the *Executive Summary* of the National Congress, we can determine how to use this good news to best implement the strategies outlined in this document.

Key to enlisting public support is telling our good news story and plan to elected officials and keeping our school highly involved in community affairs at all times. According to Dr. Charles J. O'Malley in his article "That L Word" (meaning lobbyist), Catholic schools have historically turned out well-educated, well-rounded students with sound moral values—including humility. However, unless that humility is tempered a bit, there may not be a Catholic school system. If we don't "blow our own horn," no one else will!

As principals, we know that our schools are making valuable contributions to the larger community. With a sense of calm but persistent urgency, we must get our message into the public arena. For example, if we wish our elected officials to view issues such as parental choice in education as a necessity in a free society, we must make ourselves visible to them. We must make them aware that Catholic schools offer an enriching quality education for all children.

Telling our story

We can use **direct** and **indirect** communications to spread the good news of our school. Direct communication refers to those incidents where elected officials are placed in direct contact with our students. Indirect communication refers to information which the principal, parents or board members make available to elected officials.

Direct communication. We need to invite elected officials to our school. If a picture is worth a thousand words, think of the advantages of personal contact with our students. We can let our publics experience firsthand the courtesy of our students, the orderliness of our school, the supportive and safe academic environment which is so uniquely ours. Our visitors will come away with the realization that our school is a special place as they experience the good things that are happening with our children. As self-assured principals, we will instill pride of ownership in our faculty and students. We are the best! It will be evident.

The suggestions that follow are not meant to be limiting. Many other opportunities will be effective, but these may be springboards to proclaiming our message.

Career days. Invite public officials such as city councilmen/women and state representatives to address students at specially planned activities such as career days or other such events.

Catholic Schools Week. Schedule at least one activity that includes elected officials in the celebration of Catholic education.

Senior citizen centers. Seniors love children. Schools fortunate enough to be located close to a center for senior citizens can involve students with them. These students can attend a function at which public officials will be present.

Public programs. Participate in programs made available to schools through public funds. One example is the DARE (Drug Awareness Resistance Education) Program. It is common practice to invite a long list of public officials to the DARE graduation. These events can be quite impressive and real crowd pleasers. Learn what is available through your public schools and jump on the band wagon.

Field trips. Visits to the city council and state legislature are excellent ways to make contact with your elected officials. The high visibility of your school's uniform works to your advantage.

Contests. Have students enter Civil Defense, Environmental Control or American Legion poster contests. These are fun for the children and bring local publicity.

Internship program. A number of opportunities await us here, if these programs are available in our area. Through the International Internship Program, for example, we can secure a Japanese intern for a period of six months. This participation opens the door to invite the Japanese ambassador and local officials to visit the school and view the program. This visit might be planned in conjunction with a school luncheon featuring a Japanese theme. We can let our light shine!

Indirect communication. Many other opportunities exist to let our elected officials know the fine things that are happening in our schools. We need to use that pen, word processor, fax machine, telephone, microphone...whatever is available to get our message into the mainstream.

Newsletter. The school newsletter is a natural. Parents can assist with production and distribution. Enlarge the mailing list and send the newsletter to local, state and national officials.

Grants. Let officials know what programs have been secured through grants or other assistance. If any officials have been instrumental in assisting the school, thank them and offer feedback on the project.

Student letters. Encourage students to write thank you letters after an official has visited the school.

Newspaper. Try to have articles in the local newspaper as frequently as possible. Periodically send copies of these articles with a little note to supporters. This practice will enable the school to remain visible to them.

Resources. Use available public resources. For example, one congressman has set up a teacher resource center in his local office. Send a note describing how teachers use these resources and thank him for supporting the school's efforts.

Organizations. Groups such as the Knights of Columbus and the Kiwanis Club offer various kinds of participation to students.

Lobbyists. Louisiana has a lobby group called Citizens for Educational Freedom (CEF). Such a group can contact state representatives to let them know what issues we consider important. This contact supports the efforts of our local lobbyist.

We can't be shy. We principals of Catholic schools have a beautiful story to tell. We must seize the moment. We are principals of a Catholic school at a significant time in the history of Catholic education. To paraphrase the words of Robert Frost, "We have miles to go and promises to keep before we sleep."

Resources

Catholic Schools for the 21st Century: Executive Summary, Washington, DC, NCEA, 1992.

Catholic Schools for the 21st Century: Political Action, Public Policy and Catholic Schools, Washington, DC, NCEA, 1992.

Coleman, James, *Public and Private Schools: The Impact of Communities*, New York, Basic Books, 1987.

Guerra, Donahue and Benson, *The Heart of the Matter*, Washington, DC, NCEA, 1990.

O'Malley, Charles J., "That 'L' Word," *Today's Catholic Teacher,* April 1992.

Ruth M. Frere
Holy Ghost School
Hammond, Louisiana

Carmen E. Heflin
St. Joseph School
Shreveport, Louisiana

The Spiritual Dimension of the Catholic School Board

The term spirituality has a variety of meanings in today's world. In a secular sense, it is used to express the bonding of a group or the driving force that brings people together to accomplish a goal. In a religious context, spirituality is defined as one's relationship to God, to oneself and to others.

Just as the principal is responsible for the spiritual formation of the children and faculty of a school, so too, he or she must nurture the spiritual growth of the Catholic school board. Catholic schools are faith communities. Faith and faith experiences must be the starting point from which all thinking and decision making of the board flow.

The National Congress on Catholic Schools for the 21st Century states that "the Catholic school is an integral part of the church's mission to proclaim the Gospel, build faith communities, celebrate through worship and serve others." In order to be part of this unique faith-oriented institution and to ensure that the school does promote the spiritual growth of the students, the board must recognize its own need for continuous spiritual development.

Furthermore, the board must be provided with opportunities to grow in faith and love. Eucharistic celebrations are paramount in this regard since the Eucharist is a sign of community and a cause of its growth. The board must also be provided with opportunities for prayer, reflection and for educational renewal regarding doctrine, dogma and traditions of the Catholic Church, especially contemporary documents.

Who provides these opportunities for the board? As the educational and spiritual leader, the principal is called to set the focus for the spiritual growth of the board. Theodore Drahmann and Amelia Stenger, in *The Catholic School Principal,* state that the principal provides spiritual growth opportunities for faculty, students and board members. They strongly suggest that the spiritual development of the board is a major priority of the principal.

13

Since board meetings are scheduled regularly, usually on a 10- or 12-month scale, the following action steps can be incorporated into the organizational design of the meetings:

- One or two liturgies
- A day of retreat
- Monthly prayer services
- Quarterly discussions on a particular pastoral statement

Eucharistic liturgies. All board members and their families may be invited to a celebration of Eucharist before or after the first board meeting. The theme, readings and prayer can center on the apostolic mission of the church. Later, the installation of board members can be held during a Sunday eucharistic liturgy. This could be an annual affair similar to Catechetical Sunday activities. The specific goals of the installation are:

- To mandate the mission of the board to the parish
- To provide visibility of the board as part of parish ministry
- To ask for prayers and support of the faith community for the members of the board

Day of retreat. This time for reflection may involve only the board or it may be planned in conjunction with the faculty's annual retreat day. The theme of the day could relate to the church's mission to teach and to the school's unique role in that mission. Copies of the school's vision, mission and philosophy may be given to the board for study and assimilation. The activities of the day could include input from a competent speaker, with periods of discussion relating to the mission of the church and the school.

Monthly prayer services. The monthly prayer service, planned in advance, offers an excellent opportunity to inspire and educate the board in relation to its mission, drawing themes from both the liturgical and calendar year. If the principal wants the prayer service to be meaningful, he or she formats it carefully. A suggested sequence is:

- A call to prayer (which includes reference to the theme)
- Psalm reading
- Scripture reading
- Brief reflection
- Prayer of the faithful
- Music selection

Board members are encouraged to help the principal to prepare the service and as soon as individual board members are comfortable with the planning, the principal delegates this responsibility to them. Thus the board members are able to take on another aspect of their role in forming the Catholic identity of the school.

Discussions of documents and pastoral letters. At various times, questions about the church's stance on current issues come before the board. Social justice, birth control, abortion, AIDS and euthanasia are just a few topics at the tip of the iceberg. Pastoral letters that address these issues should be provided to the board for study before the meetings. Points of concern or areas that need explanation can be addressed at the meeting by the principal or the pastor.

For example, chapters from the bishops' pastoral *Putting Children and Families First* may be assigned for meetings at which the agenda is not burdened with too many topics. This recent pastoral is pregnant with issues that are crucial for today's schools and parish communities.

September, November, January and April are good months during which to include discussions in the agenda. Limiting the discussions of documents to four times a year prevents the reading of the documents from becoming a burden to the board.

Andrew Greeley strongly recommends that the entire responsibility of operating the Catholic school be in the hands of the laity. If that should become a reality, much of the responsibility would fall to the board, demanding that board members know the apostolic mission of the church and of the school.

The board will be better prepared for this responsibility if the principal creates opportunities for board members to become persons of deep faith and firm commitment to the teachings of the church. As faithful stewards, they will be spiritual magnets drawing others to the call of the church and the mission of the school, joyfully proclaiming the gospel message, building community and giving service to all.

Resources

National Congress on Catholic Schools for the 21st Century: An Overview, Washington, DC, NCEA, 1991.

Drahmann, Theodore and Amelia Stenger, *The Catholic School Principal: An Outline for Action,* Washington, DC, NCEA, 1989.

U.S. Bishops, *Putting Children and Families First,* Washington, DC, U.S. Catholic Conference, 1991.

Aidan Hogan, OSU
St. Athanasius School
Louisville, Kentucky

The Principal and the School Board: Partnership in Student Recruitment

Quizzical looks were exchanged among St. N. School board members as they took their places around the conference table. A special meeting had been called and it seemed to portend a problem. The board president called the meeting to order and the opening prayer was said. Reports were given by the president of the home-school association, the newly hired development director, the alumni representative and, finally, the principal.

The tone of these reports, which had been in board members' hands prior to the meeting, was not optimistic. The home-school association president noted declining returns on various fund-raisers, the development director reported a lack of interest on the part of corporations to invest in an excellent technology proposal for the school, and the alumni representative said that recent phon-a-thon efforts were not successful. The principal reported that registration for the coming school year was down from the previous year. Not a happy picture!

The reality of too few students meant that St. N. School would not be cost-effective and its continuance was in danger. A study of the past five years' enrollment showed a steady decline. Nevertheless, in sharp contrast to this picture, St. N. was an academically excellent school, staffed by well-prepared and dedicated teachers and attended by motivated and well-behaved students. Furthermore, the school was assisted by committed parents, and was esteemed and supported by members of the community.

At the request of the principal, the main agenda item for this meeting was student recruitment. A very enlightening, positively directed, action-oriented discussion ensued. In previous discussions with the school board president and the pastor, the principal had realized that if the board could be instrumental in rectifying the declining enrollment, other aspects of the school's financial picture would fall into place.

The question now to be addressed was: What role does the school board, working with the principal, play in student recruitment?

The principal presented three areas to explore as background:

- The rationale for the existence/continuance of the Catholic school in general
- The problems facing Catholic schools in general and St. N.'s in particular
- The role of the school board in attracting students to St. N. School

The rationale

Following the mandate of Christ to proclaim the mystery of salvation to all peoples and to restore all things in Christ, the church is concerned with the formation of the whole person. The church participates in a dialogue with the Catholic school regarding its positive contribution to the total formation of the person.

The various church documents on education not only clarify the place of the Catholic school in the life of the church, but also reiterate the above concept. For example, the document formulated by the Congregation for Catholic Education, *The Catholic School,* states that "the absence of the Catholic school would be a great loss for civilization and for the natural and supernatural destiny of man."

In addition to the words of Christ himself, the educational community may need current research and statistics to be convinced of the importance of the Catholic school. Various researchers, both from the education and business world, presented their findings at the National Congress on Catholic Schools for the 21st Century. In summary, these findings (from *The Catholic School and Society*) are:

1) The organizational environment and general climate of Catholic schools promote student learning more than the environment of public schools.
2) Catholic schools place a stronger emphasis on academics and have more demanding academic requirements than do public schools.
3) Catholic school teachers rate their students higher in cooperation, motivation, discipline and school interest than public school teachers rate their students.
4) Parents of Catholic schools students have higher expectations for their children and monitor the work of their children more than do parents of public school children.

At this point in the meeting, school board members had a look of "Doesn't everyone know this?...We do!" on their faces. The principal continued the presentation.

Problems of continuance

The problem faced by St. N. School, as well as by Catholic schools across the nation, is a decline in enrollment. In 1990, more than 3 million fewer children attended Catholic schools than in 1964. A greatly reduced birth rate among Catholic families contributed to this decline in enrollment. However, a significant part of the decline resulted from a sharp decrease in the number of Catholic parents who sent their children to Catholic schools.

The reasons for this are varied: the rising cost of Catholic school tuition heightened by the strained finances of families; lack of a conveniently located Catholic school in the area; doubts about the school's ability to offer a quality academic program in poorer facilities and in larger classes than those of the neighboring public schools.

Also, in some Catholic schools, the parish priest and the local bishop no longer present Catholic school attendance as a serious obligation, thereby implying to the laity an indifference to the intrinsic value of the institution.

Scanning the faces of the school board, the principal could see some eyebrows still raised, waiting for the answer to the dilemma to be presented. Others nodded in understanding and agreement, while still others had the "aha" moment written on their faces. This was the group that the principal hoped would now be a catalyst in the ensuing discussion.

Recruiting new students

The principal remarked that perhaps she seemed to be presenting a great deal of theory to get to the practical, but she felt that the board needed to be well informed about the facts in order to formulate some action statements.

The first "aha" person to speak came from a large family, all of whom had attended St. N. School, and was the mother of four children currently attending the school. She suggested that the public (parents, parishioners, Catholic parents in neighboring parishes) needed to hear the "good news" about Catholic schools from those members of the school community who are highly visible—the pastor, the principal, the members of the board.

("We're getting there," smiled the principal to herself.) The other board members came alive now and suggestions abounded in quick succession:

"How about the pastor featuring the Catholic schools in a homily or in the church bulletin?"

"Couldn't the principal speak about the school at various weekend liturgies? Couldn't the principal go out to the feeder parishes with a board member to speak about the school, then be available after Mass to distribute school brochures and answer questions people may have about the school?"

"Couldn't we get information about tuition, busing, academic excellence into the hands of the local realtors by asking the home-school association to sponsor a realtors' breakfast and have board members on hand to give a tour of the school?"

"We have an attractively designed brochure. Why are we waiting to distribute it to parents after they have enrolled their children at St. N. School? Couldn't one of us, along with the principal, visit the local realtors when they have their monthly meeting and go over the brochure with them?"

"Couldn't we ask the home-school association, which has a publicity committee, to get the "good news" to the media about St. N. School? After all, we are influential people. Can't we help by taking an editor (or a realtor) to lunch and, over a pleasant meal, share with him/her our own positive experience at St. N. School?"

"What does the appearance of our school say to those considering St. N. School for the first time? We have a building and grounds committee on the parish council. Let's suggest that they 'spruce up' the place, inside and out. After all, a child and his/her parents should feel proud of the appearance of the school!"

"And you know, despite the obvious, many people still don't even know where our school is located. We should really pursue the possibility of getting a sign out on the front lawn as well as right on the building."

"Have we missed any group that could help? Of course, the two groups that form an integral part of the school—teachers and students! Do we have teachers who, by their very stance, convey the message of "good news"? Development experts tell us that the entry level teachers are the best advertisement for the school. Are they professionally well prepared, sensitive to the needs of the children, and imbued with gospel values?"

"Are our students happy? Nothing sells a product better than satisfied customers!"

"How will we as school board members, selected by the school community with pastor and principal approval, witness to our belief in Catholic schools in general and to our school in particular?"

"I've heard of a program called 'Bear-ly Recruiting' in the Metuchen Diocese in New Jersey. It seems that grade two students send cards to the newly baptised children of the parish. Each year, that same child sends the youngster a birthday card. Finally, on the child's fifth birthday, he/she receives a 'Welcome to School' coloring book. Seems like a great PR idea!"

"Along with that, I read somewhere that NCEA puts out little T-shirts imprinted with the Catholic Schools Week logo to be given to the newly baptised children."

"Speaking of PR, couldn't we work together to have our gym uniforms screen printed with our school name? Everywhere the students go, St. N. School names will be before the public."

Neither the board president nor the principal expected such a barrage of ideas and the concomitant excitement. It was nearly 10 p.m. Clearly, such an important issue could only be presented at this meeting. After drawing up a checklist of tasks to be done by various members of the school community (see Appendix), the meeting was adjourned. The fulfillment of these tasks lay ahead, but the time was ripe for their initiation.

Resources

Abbott, Walter M. (ed.), "Declaration on Christian Education," *The Documents of Vatican II,* New York, Guild Press, 1966.

Brigham, Frederick, John Convey and John Cummins, *The Catholic School and Society,* Washington, DC, NCEA, 1991.

Buetow, Harold A., *A History of United States Catholic Schooling,* Washington, DC, NCEA, 1985.

Congregation for Catholic Education, *The Catholic School,* Boston, Daughters of St. Paul, 1977.

Guerra, Michael, Regina Haney and Robert Kealey, *National Congress on Catholic Schools for the 21st Century: Executive Summary,* Washington, DC, NCEA, 1992.

Heft, James and Carleen Reck, *The Catholic Identity of Catholic Schools,* Washington, DC, NCEA, 1991.

O'Brien, J. Stephen, *Mixed Messages: What Bishops and Priests Say About Catholic Schools,* Washington, DC, NCEA, 1987.

Tabert, Eileen, *Bear-ly Recruiting,* Diocese of Metuchen, NJ, 1989.

Appendix
Student Recruitment Checklist

_____Pastor   Feature school at parish liturgies
              Feature school in church bulletins

21

_____Principal	Speak at neighboring parishes Visit local realtors Attend realtors breakfast Investigate Bear-ly Recruiting program Investigate NCEA T-shirts Investigate gym uniforms with school name
_____Home-School Association	Sponsor realtors breakfast Contact media Take an editor/realtor to lunch
_____Parish Council	Assess building and grounds of school Pursue building of signs on grounds and on building
_____Teachers	Acquaint teachers with idea that they are marketers of the school
_____Board	Coordinate activities of all of the above

M. Joseph Spring, SCC
St. Joseph School
Mendham, New Jersey

Section II
Public Policy

The Principal and the School Board: Getting Into Politics

"As the principal goes, so goes the board." What a wonderful way to describe the nature of school boards in our Catholic schools. As much as we may hesitate to believe it, the board's development, its successes or attempts to succeed are directly related to the principal's work with them.

One area of the board's responsibilities that needs to be developed in conjunction with the principal, especially in schools and parishes with many financial burdens, is their relationship with the legislature. Since local boards are generally regarded as most responsible for making decisions regarding school finances, these boards must make contact with legislative bodies to make known the needs of the students in their schools.

Board members should be involved in the political arena of choice and justice in education. They should be willing to use their political savvy to obtain the resources needed for schools. It is imperative that board members and all parents be registered voters and actively participate in voting. Board members need to involve taxpayers. They can help parents lobby for choice in the education of their children.

Where to begin

In getting the board involved politically, I recommend that the members first view the National Congress video, which specifically addresses the role boards can play in local political action. Principals can contact their diocesan offices of education or the NCEA directly to obtain a copy of the video.

This viewing will help "stir into flame," as Dr. Robert Kealey says, the inspiration boards need to undertake the task of political involvement. After viewing the video, some board members may be willing to form a public policy committee.

25

A model initiative

At the time of this writing, a GI Bill for Children has been presented by President Bush to the House and Senate. It is a good example of the kind of legislation to which boards should give their full support. In this bill, half-a-billion new federal dollars would be given to help states and communities provide each child of a middle- and low-income family with a $1000 annual scholarship to any lawfully operating school of their choice—public, private or religious. Up to $500 of each scholarship could be used for other academic programs for children before and after school, on weekends, and during school vacations. As stated in the *Wall Street Journal,* this program is evidence that empowering parents with some choice is an idea whose time has come.

I suggest that boards spend part of one of their meetings discussing a parent choice program such as this. Members of the board should send letters to their state representatives and senators who support parent choice and to the president and secretary of education, informing them of their full support of parent choice programs. The board could also begin a write-in campaign or a phone-a-thon at their parish during which board members would encourage parishoners and school parents to contact their congresspersons.

Continuing efforts

Initiating a campaign which supports parental choice programs and which prompts the board to contact their elected state officials will motivate the board to continue to invest their energy and time. The board also can encourage the modification of tax law so as to provide relief to parents.

What about tax vouchers? Are Chapter I services really best serving the children? Strong ongoing action on the part of the board is crucial if any progress toward redesigning methods of federal aid to our schools is to occur. The activity of the board must not be just a one-shot effort. The principal must continue to inform board membership of political happenings in the education field and to encourage their involvement.

The challenge is for the principal to be aware of legislative happenings and to report these to the board. The principal can keep current on the issues through reading the daily newspaper and *Education Week,* as well as communications from the state Catholic Conference. He or she can then provide background reports for the board to discuss current trends which involve Catholic education, e.g., the National Congress, and invite local and state representatives or a diocesan official familiar with workings at the state level to address the board.

Resources

Building Better Boards Handbook, Washington, DC, NCEA, 1990.

National Congress on Catholic Schools for the 21st Century: Catholic School Governance and Finance, Washington, DC, NCEA, 1991.

National Congress on Catholic Schools for the 21st Century: Political Action, Public Policy and Catholic Schools, Washington, DC, NCEA, 1991.

Paula C. DeKeersgieter
All Souls School
St. Louis, Missouri

Policial Action: The Practical Role of the Principal

Remember the "good old days" when the role of the principal was restricted to being the instructional and spiritual leader? Not any more! Our role has expanded and we now wear many more hats. Scott D. Thomson, executive secretary for the National Policy Board for Educational Administration, states:

> No longer is it enough to be managers of routines. Principals need increasingly to take initiatives. They must involve and motivate staff, create a positive culture, build a group vision, develop quality educational programs, provide a positive instructional environment, encourage high performance, apply an evaluation process, analyze and interpret outcomes, be accountable for results, and maximize human resources.

We are the visionaries for not only our schools, but also for future generations.

Shout it out

It is no longer acceptable for us to concern ourselves with just the "here and now." We have to take an active public stance in regard to all areas of education. We need to communicate with, motivate and lead our faculties, parents, school boards, alumni associations and the entire school community so that they will raise their voices in a common cause—our children. We need to become involved in political action.

Political action is not a new term, but it is unfamiliar and even intimidating to some of us. We are often caught in the middle of the debate between church and state. Participating in political actions doesn't affect the church; it affects the right of equal benefits to which our children are entitled.

One of our recent challenges has been to publicize the good news of Catholic education. As Lourdes Sheehan, RSM, states, "Public relations is both an art and a science. As an art, it enables people to understand the school....It is the science of selecting the appropriate media, materials, and events to connect effectively with audiences with which the school wishes to establish good will."

How do we get our message or position across? It is important that we get media coverage both on political actions favoring our stance and on those that could have an adverse affect on our efforts. In our experience, media attention, whether it be through television or print, has a great impact.

As Sister Lourdes states, "One can characterize public relations as the sum of all that a school or a person does or does not do which affects how it is perceived and supported by various groups or publics in a community."

Divide and conquer

The political arena is an important and influential area, but it has been ignored by school administrators for too many years. Catholic school principals need to lead the Catholic community in accepting the challenge and responsibility of becoming involved in political action and public policy. One of those new hats for us to wear! We need to make a conscious effort to devote the necessary time to meeting this challenge.

Time management will play an important part in this challenge. Initially, the principal will spend much of his/her time becoming informed on public policy related to educational concerns on both the local and national levels. A plan must be initiated by the principal in collaboration with his/her human resources. These resources can be tapped into to accomplish our goals of communication, motivation and action with the Catholic community.

Who are these human resources? Pastor, faculty, staff, school board, parents, parish and alumni associations are our assets. Among them, furthermore, may be persons who are related to or who know people on the political front.

"Divide and conquer" is essential to the scheme of our plan. Delegation to key individuals on political issues means that each person does not need to address every issue. This is where a check and balance system works well.

Members of the school board, parent association and alumni association can be utilized to steer a political advocacy committee. The goal of this committee is to act on behalf of all the people in the school community. The committee will advocate on behalf of the school when an issue is presented on a local, state or federal level. Members of the steering committee would be responsible for:

- Investigating and communicating one specific issue
- Recruiting individuals from within and outside the community willing to serve on the political advocacy committee
- Organizing letter writing, making phone calls and/or personal visits to politicians involved in legislation

Action words for collaboration

Dialogue between the steering committee and our office must never break down. We must **trust** the steering committee to keep us informed of daily happenings in the legislation, and **encourage** members of the advocacy committee to attend the hearings and debates.

As we **communicate** with our political representatives, we need to let them know that we were there and to comment both on the stance that they took at the hearings and where we stand on an issue.

We must **involve** the media. Letters to the editors are always effective in getting our message across. We can **utilize** local radio talk shows to reach a wider audience concerning our position, as well as newsletters written to the school community and parish to prompt swift action in favor of our stand.

Our task includes **educating** the community at large. We can no longer afford to be conformists. We need to get out of the mode of the 1950s and 60s, when we sat back and hoped that someone was looking out for our interests. Too many large interest groups are working against the issues that directly affect our children.

Our committee can **circulate** an updated list of all senators and representatives. Since many parents live outside our school district, they should be asked to check their voter registration cards to determine their district.

Although we need to **provide** guidelines for phone calls/personal visits and the dos and don'ts of legislative writing (see Appendices A and B), we should avoid sending home a sample letter. These form letters are ranked very low when it comes to influencing legislative opinion. Letters that are thoughtful and sincere and directly affect the writer get the most attention. These letters are often quoted in committee hearings or in debate.

Along with the steering committee, we need to **communicate** the fact that getting involved in political action directly affects not only this generation of children, but also the next generation. Adults need to **model** to their children the acceptability of taking risks in a constructive way. Our present generation of children are very aware of issues affecting today's world.

The next generation

One important public policy questions is: Where has all the money gone for educational assistance? Some students may know the answer better than we do. We can encourage them to enter essay contests and to participate in projects related to this question and other public policy issues.

Since their concerns tend to go along with what they hear constantly on the news, they may need our help in setting priorities. For example, in 1992 the environment was on students' minds in issues such as pollution, recycling, rain forests and the ozone. We realize that we need to do something about these issues so we'll have our students around to be the leaders of tomorrow.

But do we compromise too many dollars on these issues that could be used more wisely in the basic education our youth? That would be a price we can't afford to pay. Keeping long-range goals in mind, students need to maximize their creative and problem-solving skills so we will be able to solve this and many other problems, such as drugs, alcohol and crime.

Young people cannot get a good education if their parents don't help. This is especially true when it comes to political action. Adults must be urged to take the initiative to help preserve or change public policies that will directly affect their child's life.

President John F. Kennedy stated in his inaugural address that "a nation's most valuable resource is its children." To protect this resource, we must accept the challenge and responsibility to lead the Catholic community in addressing educational legislation and public policy. We will be held accountable by our children and their children for the way their future has been shaped.

Resources

Sheehan, Lourdes, *Building Better Boards Handbook,* Washington, DC, NCEA, 1990.

Thomson, Scott D., "A New Kind of Principal," *Agenda*, Winter 1992.

Appendix A
Phone Calls/Personal Visits to Political Leaders

- Try calling/visiting your legislator person-to-person, especially if you have previously corresponded with him/her; otherwise, ask for the staff person handling the issue of interest.
- Identify yourself and the school on whose behalf you are calling.
- If you have corresponded with him/her, make mention of it

or refer to it.
- Keep your calls brief and to the point.
- Be sure to call in advance for an appointment. Arrive on time but be understanding if you are kept waiting.
- Be well prepared and accurate. Know as much as possible about the topic you wish to discuss.
- Be sure any information you plan to leave with your legislator is neat and concise.
- Be polite. Calmly explain your points and help your legislator to understand the reasons for your point of view. Allow your legislator to fully respond to your points and thank him/her for his/her ideas. Do not get into an argument.
- Limit your visit to 10 or 15 minutes and leave on a friendly note.
- Keep a log or a journal of phone calls or personal visits noting:
  — the date of the call or the visit
  — the position that the politician holds
  — details that you can build upon to make a stronger case
  — follow-up date for further contact
- Follow through!

Appendix B
Do's and Don'ts of Legislative Writing
DO:
- Address your state legislator properly.

Envelope	**Salutation**
United States Senator:	
Honorable John Doe	Dear Senator Doe:
United States Senate	
Washington, DC 20510-4703	
United States Representative:	
Honorable John Doe	Dear Congresswoman Doe:
United States House of	or
Representatives	Dear Congressman Doe:
Washington, DC 20515-1101	
State Senator:	
Honorable John Doe	Dear Senator Doe:
State Senate	
State House	
Capital, State, Zip	

State Representative:
Honorable John Doe   Dear Mr. Doe:
House of Representatives   or
State House   Dear Representative Doe:
Capital, State, Zip

Governor:
The Honorable John Doe   Dear Governor Doe:
State House
Capitol, State, Zip

- Write legibly (handwritten letters are fine if they are readable).

- Be brief and to the point; discuss only one issue in each letter; identify a bill by number and title if possible.

- Use your own words and your own stationary. If you are writing as the representative of a group, use the organization's stationary.

- Include your address and sign your name legibly. If you have any family, business or political connection in regard to the issue, explain it. It may serve as an identification when your point of view is considered.

- Be courteous and reasonable.

- Write when your legislator does something of which you approve. Legislators hear mostly from constituents who are against something; this gives them a one-sided picture of their constituency. A note of appreciation will make your legislator remember you favorably the next time you write.

- Write before a bill has been introduced if you have some ideas that you would like to see included in legislation. If you are lobbying for or against a bill and your legislator is a member of the committee to which it has been referred, write when the committee begins hearings. If your legislator is not a member of the committee handling the bill, write just before the bill is to come to the floor for debate and vote.

- Write the chairman or members of a committee holding hearings if you wish, but remember that you have more influence with legislators from your own district than with any others.

- Write the governor/president after the bill is passed by both houses if you want to influence the decision to sign the bill or not.

DON'T:
- Write on a postcard.

- Sign and send a form letter.

- Begin on the righteous note of "As a citizen and taxpayer."

- Apologize for writing and taking their time. If your letter is short and expresses your opinion, they are glad to give you a hearing.

- Be rude or threatening. It will get you nowhere.

- Be vague. Some letters are written in such general terms that they leave the legislator wondering what in the world the writer had in mind.

- Send a carbon copy to your other legislators when you have addressed the letter to one. Write each one individually.

- Write to the members of the House while a bill is being considered in the Senate and vice versa. The bill may be quite changed before it leaves the chamber.

These appendices are modeled after materials developed by the Catholic Schools Office, Joliet, Illinois, 1992.

Kathleen M. Adams
Cranston-Johnston Catholic Regional School
Cranston, Rhode Island

Ellen C. Herron
Holy Family School
Joliet, Illinois

Communicating Public Policy

The principal needs to assess the communication vehicles to be used in order to enhance education regarding specific public policy issues and to encourage the involvement of parents and school board members.

Well-rounded relationships are the foundation for good communication. In preparing the school community to be receptive to what needs to be said about a specific issue, the principal first asks questions of himself/herself, such as:
- Do I know how to relate well with my clientele?
- Am I prepared to address this public policy issue effectively?
- What approach is best to make my presentation interesting?
- What resources do I have to share with my audience?

The principal can then provide the necessary background on the issue to be addressed. This sets the stage for clarification, collaboration and support in developing a response to the issue. Parents and members of the school board are then brought together to take a stand on behalf of quality education.

President Bush's GI Bill for Children is just one example of a public policy issue about which parents and members of the school board must be kept informed and highly motivated to support. The principal's task is threefold: keeping current, informing others and motivating the school community to action.

Keeping current
How does the principal keep him/herself and others current? The principal is made aware of specific public policies affecting the school community in a variety of ways. Among them are:
- Open communication with the superintendent

- Educational newsletters
- Periodic databases such as CONNECT
- Local and national newspapers

Other sources of educational public policy are obtained through the state Catholic Conference, the United States Catholic Conference, the National Catholic Educational Association, local officials and others.

Informing others

It is the responsibility of the principal to communicate, as quickly and as effectively as possible, this information to the parents and school board members, alerting them to the importance of their involvement in the legislative process so that together they can make a difference.

Parents and board members are the first ones to be informed. The clearer the purpose of the vehicle of communication for each of the various policy issues, the better the school community will respond. The following are some of the means used to disseminate information:

- A video highlighting the most important aspects of the policy issue
- Use of weekly school bulletins
- Use of the PTG newsletter
- Information on school bulletin boards
- Word of mouth
- Invitation to a state legislator who supports a public policy issue to address parents and school board members
- Church bulletin
- News media

Follow-up reports on the progress of a policy will be shared with the school community on a regular basis. This ongoing dissemination of information is meant to keep everyone current and interested in doing his/her share on behalf of the school.

Motivating to action

In order to keep parents and school boards highly motivated to do their share, a strong sense of community must be encouraged among them. The principal will make use of every opportunity to affirm their role as transformer agents in their quest for excellence. An understanding of the importance of their involvement is a key element in nurturing motivation.

Members of the school community who are lawyers and/or politicians can be recruited to share their knowledge and expertise in this endeavor of motivating to action. Open communication generates interest and involvement.

A well-organized public policy committee can also assist the principal to keep current, inform and motivate parents and school board members. This committee will be made up of the following members:
- The school principal
- A lawyer
- A public relations chairperson
- A parent from each ethnic group
- Other people as needed

One way to highlight the importance of getting the school community involved is to keep a chart of attendance at public policy meetings. The class whose parents have shown up for these meetings will be granted service credit. The children whose parents have 100% attendance will be given a special privilege such as a free dress day. If the specific measure/legislation gets to its final stage with victory on the school's behalf, the principal will host a celebration pot-luck dinner for the entire school.

In conclusion, the principal will make use of his/her knowledge and public relations skills to provide the parents and members of the school board not only with the information they need to learn about the implications of public policy issues but, by so doing, he/she also will pave the road for change and ownership of Catholic education.

Resources

Catholic Schools for the 21st Century: Executive Summary, Washington, DC, NCEA, 1992.

Council for American Private Education, "GI Bill for Children Reignites Choice Debate," *Cape Outlook,* September 1992.

Menicucci, David F., *Catholic Home and School Association Guidebook,* Washington, DC, NCEA, 1990.

Julia Dias Fonseca, FHIC
Five Wounds School
San Jose, California

Networking for Public Policy Issues

With the dwindling of already scarce financial resources, educational administrators must turn to a collaborative effort with the broader educational community to strategize on public policy issues and to lobby national and state legislative bodies for a fair share of government educational funding dollars.

Efforts to mobilize support for public policy issues in the past relied totally upon the local superintendent and principals. This method of reaching parents and voters has become increasingly ineffective over the last 12 years. Catholic school administrators often do not have the clerical support staff nor the time to support the networking that is necessary for effective action.

Nevertheless, before looking at a model of a state coalition organized to influence public policy and legislative processes, it may be helpful to note some means now open to Catholic school administrators seeking to influence public policy issues.

Local school model

Write and call federal and state education directors, policy-making groups and political representatives for information. If a newsletter and other materials which discuss current issues are available, ask to be placed on the mailing list.

Attend federal and state meetings and conferences on specific topics. Participate and bring back the information through the established network.

Attend or form political issue groups. Attend political issue groups within your state, district, county, diocese or local community as a start. When you are unable to find a group that deals with the issues

41

in which you are most interested, the alternative is to create one. This is not as ambitious as it may sound at first. The trick is to select one or two persons in the school or parish community, influential people who are also interested in the issue, and form such an issue group. Suggest they contact other parent, educator and community groups.

Join advisory groups that formulate issue statements at the federal and state levels.

Look at local programs that the federal, state or districts may be calling "models" or "model" programs.

Invite federal, state and local politically elected officials to address superintendents and principals.

Acquire and study subject-specific materials such as videos, cassettes, books, periodicals, monographs and manuals, and distribute them to other administrators. These materials are available through many sources. Among the most common are ERIC Clearinghouse and educational publications' reference lists available in public libraries. These references usually cite periodicals that trace the history of the subject and provide the reader with the most current information.

Subscribe to educational journals. Most educators find it almost impossible to keep up with the abundance of information generated about public policy issues related to education or educational institutions. How then do principals do all that is expected of them and still keep up with what is going on in this area?

The answer is: Read selectively. Almost all journals attend to specific populations and few attempt to cover the broad range of public policy issues. Subscriptions to these journals usually include newsletters and other useful information such as legislation updates.

Organizations that publish public issue newsletters or journal articles include:
- National Catholic Educational Association (NCEA) membership includes the journal *Momentum* and the newsletter *NCEA Notes.*
- The National Association of Boards of Catholic Education (NABE), a commission of NCEA, membership includes *Issue-Gram*, published twice a year. All board members receive the newsletter.
- Phi Delta Kappa (PDK) membership includes the newsletter *Phi Delta Kappa Legislative Newsletter: A View From the Hill.*

- Newsletters such as *Education Weekly* and *Education Today* are available from private publishers.

Utilize the services that are currently available. State Catholic Conference newsletters, diocesan-superintendent notes and meetings, public school system superintendent notes, state education department memorandums, and Catholic Television Network videos are but a few of the existing services available in many states.

Some dioceses and districts have made available to their local administrators an interactional electronic network called CONNECT. This allows subscribers to access information via satellite on a variety of topics, using the computer and modem. Administrators in those dioceses not yet connected to electronic networks will find that the methods listed above are adequate but not as quick or selective.

Catholic school administrators relying upon means such as those described above may wish to investigate the viability of a statewide network to increase their ability to influence public policy and legislative decisions.

State coalition model

The state of Indiana has developed a model that has served all nonpublic schools for the past seven years. This is totally a school administrator's network. The components of this type of network are:

Nonpublic school positions are represented in the legislature. Specific representatives and senators speak for you in party caucuses and in committees on the floor. Those groups which can influence decision making often rely less on grass-roots efforts but are most effective with both.

A paid lobbyist carries your message on a daily basis into the halls and to committee presentations. For example, the Indiana Non-Public Principals Education Administration (INPEA), through its state organization, hires a director/lobbyist to plead the cause of all non-public schools in Indiana. The organization's membership includes Catholic, Lutheran, Christian, Jewish, Adventist, Baptist and private schools. The organization has local level groups and meetings.

Influentials are identified. An influential is a person who has access to a legislator.

A relationship between lobbyists and the networkers is developed and structured. Existing structures are followed where possible. Each diocesan school superintendent appoints a staff person to receive action alerts from the lobbyist. That alert is transmitted to a building contact appointed by the building principal. The building principal or contact alerts subgroup contacts (faculty, parents, students) who proceed to activate the small phone alert networks.

Once your alert chain has been developed, local contacts should familiarize the local networkers with names, addresses and phone numbers of legislators serving the voting area where the school is located.

The National Congress on Catholic Schools for the 21st Century states as one of its goals on political action, public policy and Catholic schools the need "to convene an assembly of key leaders in Catholic schooling as well as appropriate representatives of researchers, business and public officials in order to create strategies for the future of the schools." It is time to renew efforts, reinvigorate commitment and revitalize leadership at the national, state and local levels.

The challenge to the Catholic school community is to find the necessary time and resources to develop a viable grass-roots and/or statewide organization of Catholic and private school parents which can effectively impact the public and legislative processes for favorable treatment at the national, state and local levels. Two models have been presented here.

Barbara K. McClure
Saint Joseph's School
Decatur, Indiana

Building a Coalition for Public Policy

Is public policy an educational buzzword that means little or nothing to the school principal?

Is public policy just one of many equally important areas of study and involvement for the busy administrator?

Is public policy the concern solely of the bishop and superintendent?

The answer to all three questions is a resounding "no"! Principals and parents, bishops and superintendents, working in a cohesive manner but as distinctly recognizable groups, can give Catholic schools a strong posture for legislative success. Each group brings a unique message to state legislators. Powerful coalitions of Catholic and other nonpublic school systems, as well as other interested allies, are necessary in order to overcome enormously powerful public school lobbyists.

In the Public Policy paper of the National Congress on Catholic Schools for the 21st Century, the author identified 19 such groups that may wish to join Catholic school coalitions. The more widespread the participation, the better the opportunity to identify and recruit allies.

This report will detail a model plan used in New York. If you do not have a state organization for superintendents, principals and parents, and this plan appears to have value, please share it with your superintendent and fellow principals. Your own and other state dioceses can then consider the plan for the state. As with many successful projects, your public policy coalition may start at a grassroots level.

New York State Plan for a Public Policy Network for Catholic Schools

Objective:

The Public Policy Education Network for Catholic Schools is intended to mobilize the Catholic school community statewide behind legislation that would benefit Catholic school students and parents.

Structure and Function:

State Coordinating Committee (SCC): The SCC is composed of the following representatives: two each from the Catholic Council of School Superintendents, Federation of Catholic School Parents, Catholic School Administrators Organization; one each from the New York State Catholic Conference, New York State Knights of Columbus; one diocesan coordinator from each diocese; ex officio, the executive directors/secretaries of the superintendents', principals' and parents' state association.

The SCC is responsible for developing and overseeing the implementation of a statewide action plan to realize legislative objectives approved by the State Catholic Conference and other member organizations. It is chaired by a person elected by members of the coordinating committee for a two-year, renewable term. It meets at least twice a year, but more frequently if deemed appropriate by the members.

State Coordinator: The executive secretary of the Council of Catholic School Superintendents serves as state coordinator and is responsible for:
- developing for approval by the SCC initial drafts of action plans for achieving legislative objectives;
- implementing and monitoring at the state level the action plans approved by the SCC;
- developing support materials for local implementation of the action plans;
- determining day-to-day policy and strategy consistent with the overall policy and strategy approved by the SCC;
- coordinating interactions with legislators, government officials and various organizations at the state and national levels;
- serving as executive secretary of the SCC;
- gathering and distributing information and other data necessary for dealing with legislators.

Diocesan Coordinator: The diocesan coordinator is appointed by the diocesan superintendent of schools and is responsible for:
- implementing and monitoring the statewide action plans at

the diocesan level;
- identifying, convening and training all regional coordinators, legislative district coordinators and school-level coordinators;
- serving as a two-way link in the communication chain between the SCC and the school coordinators, legislative district coordinators and diocesan communications channels;
- establishing and maintaining an instant action phone network within the diocese;
- linking with the diocesan coordinator for the State Catholic Conference's Public Policy Education Network to ensure coordinated efforts and to utilize that network in pursuit of legislative objectives relating to Catholic schools;
- establishing and convening, as necessary, a diocesan coordinating committee (optional).

Legislative District Coordinator: The legislative district coordinator is identified by the diocesan coordinator. There should be one coordinator for each assembly district that has a school within the diocese. Some of those coordinators would then also be asked to serve as coordinators for the larger legislative districts in which they are

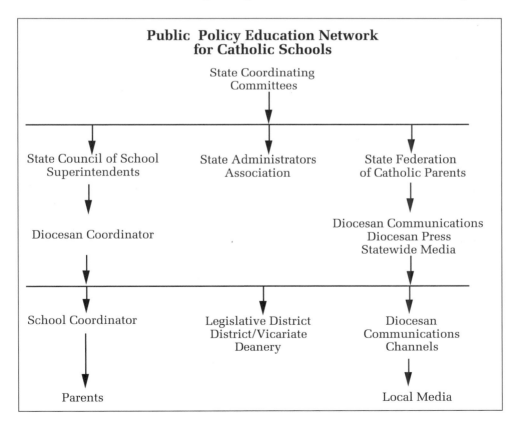

Public Policy Education Network for Catholic Schools

State Coordinating Committees

State Council of School Superintendents

State Administrators Association

State Federation of Catholic Parents

Diocesan Coordinator

Diocesan Communications
Diocesan Press
Statewide Media

School Coordinator

Legislative District
District/Vicariate
Deanery

Diocesan
Communications
Channels

Parents

Local Media

47

located (e.g., state senate districts and congressional districts).

Because of the great number of assembly districts in some dioceses, it may be necessary to identify a level of coordinators higher than assembly district coordinators, e.g., regional or county coordinators, in order to make the network more manageable. This is entirely a matter of diocesan discretion.

The legislative district coordinator is responsible for:
- implementing and monitoring the statewide action plan at the legislative district level;
- establishing and maintaining an instant action phone network within the legislative district;
- identifying appropriate persons (e.g., parents, pastors, principals, influential leaders within the community) who could serve as spokespersons with the legislators;
- organizing visits and meetings with the legislator;
- ensuring that regular communications are maintained with the legislator and his/her staff;
- reporting back to appropriate coordinators regarding the position of the legislator on the issues involved;
- establishing and convening, as necessary, a legislative district coordinating committee (optional).

School Coordinator: The school coordinator is appointed by the school principal. There should be one school coordinator for each school within the diocese. The school coordinator is responsible for:
- implementing and monitoring the statewide action plan at the school level;
- ensuring that action alerts are distributed to parents and parishioners, working with the parish coordinator for the Catholic Conference's Public Policy Network, if such a person has been identified;
- establishing and maintaining an instant action phone network within the school community;
- reporting back to appropriate coordinators regarding the position of legislators on the issues involved;
- establishing and convening, as necessary, a school coordinating committee (optional)

* * *

What is the role of the principal in this statewide plan for a public policy network? The four major responsibilities of the principal are to:
- encourage the idea of state administrator and parents associations;
- give the association financial support;

- suggest the names of people and groups who might assist the Catholic schools in forming broad coalitions;
- follow through on action steps (phone calls, letters, visits to offices) when asked by a state conference.

Through the formation of such broad-based coalitions, Catholic schools may finally experience public policy success in state capitols. The goal of such groups is clear and specific: that government finally assume its responsibility to support the educational needs of all students and all parents.

John J. Burke
Saint Thomas Aquinas School
Bronx, New York

In Support of School Choice

The National Congress on Catholic Schools for the 21st Century, a jointly planned venture of three departments of the National Catholic Educational Association, has revitalized and renewed the climate of commitment to the future of Catholic schooling in the United States.

The delegates to the National Congress promulgated the following belief statements on Political Action, Public Policy and Catholic Schools:

We believe that:
- Democratic principles demand that all parents have a right to choose appropriate education for their children and to receive a fair share of education tax dollars to exercise that right.
- Federal, state and local level political action involving the total Catholic community is essential to protect the rights of all students and parents.
- Advocacy for low-income families is essential to tax-supported parental choice in education.
- Coalitions are essential for successful political action.
- Tax-supported systems of educational choice can improve all schools.

Since federal, state and local level political action is essential, principals need to keep up-to-date personally, and to inform and motivate parents and members of school boards about issues affecting their schools. This paper is an attempt to share some ideas and proposals about today's most challenging and current struggle—the issue of choice legislation!

The rationale

According to the NCEA publication *Catholic Schools in America 1992,* the number of Catholic schools has decreased in the last decade by 10% and the number of students served in that time has decreased by 16% despite increasing evidence of the effectiveness of Catholic schools. These facts indicate the need for a plan to revitalize and strengthen existing schools and expand the network of Catholic schools in our country.

In our competitive society we are constantly trying to improve everything, from our figure or face to our golf or tennis swing. Business is constantly researching ways to improve their products: finding a better taste, a fresher fragrance, a thicker sauce or more snap, crackle and pop. Businesses compete to develop products that are lowest in sodium, fat or sugar.

Cannot this same striving for excellence be applied to education in order to produce graduates who excel academically?

Today many families shop for schools before they shop for homes. For those who can choose and afford the best home, a choice of schools is also possible. Often poorer housing means poorer public schools. We have learned from business that choice and competition ultimately produce the most affordable excellent product.

It would follow that a choice for parents in educational institutions would also offer an affordable excellent academic institution, for the marketplace does separate the good from the less good.

Educational choice can promote academic excellence by fostering basic reforms and creating a competitive climate, one responsive to parental concerns and leading to improved student performance. Choice will also return to parents their primary right of educating their children in the setting of their choice.

In addition, parents can demand more accountability from the educational institution of their choice. The choice system encourages decentralization, site-based management, respect for teachers and principals, professionalism, close relations with families, and programs of excellence designed to meet the specific needs and learning goals of students.

The present situation concerning choice legislation is stirring on at least four fronts: nationally, at the state level, in several cities, and with privately funded initiatives. Catholic school communities can also initiate ways to support school choice.

Federal initiatives

One example of action at the nation level is the GI Bills for Children announced by President Bush on June 25, 1992. The bill would give children of low- or middle-income families a $1000 annual scholarship that families could spend at any lawfully operating school of their choice—public, private or church-related.

Under this proposed legislation, the state or locality would establish its definition of middle- and low-income levels. This would be subject to a cap based on the higher of either the state or national median family income, according to the U.S. Department of Education.

To receive federal funding, the state or locality would have to permit families to spend the $1000 scholarships at a wide variety of public and private schools and allow all lawfully operating schools in the area—public, private and church-related—to participate if they choose.

Michael Guerra, executive director of the secondary schools department of NCEA, called the GI Bills for Children "the most important education legislation since Lyndon Johnson's Elementary and Secondary Education Act in 1965."

Dr. Robert Kealey, executive director of the elementary schools department of NCEA, said, "Low- and middle-income families who cannot afford to live in the best neighborhoods with the best public schools now will have an opportunity to exercise a right the rich have always had—choosing schools for their youngsters."

State initiatives

The Wall Street Journal of February 27, 1992, reported the following states as considering or having acted on proposals to allow the use of taxpayer money toward private-school tuition. In Alabama, Florida, Illinois, Oregon, Pennsylvania and West Virginia, the legislations have proposed some form of statewide private school voucher program. In California, backers have tried to put an initiative on the ballot for a statewide private school voucher program. In Maryland and Wisconsin, legislators have tried to design a low-income voucher program.

City/privately funded initiatives

In Milwaukee a plan was developed by the city to give vouchers to poor families to send their children to private schools. Businesses in Indianapolis are providing vouchers to enable low-income students to choose private schools.

Mr. J. Patrick Rooney, chairman of the board of the Golden Rule Insurance Co., said,"I didn't see anything happening in the near future on educational choice. So we decided we'd do something." The insurance company offered $1.2 million in vouchers to help low-income parents cover the cost of sending their children to any of Indianapolis' private and parochial schools.

School initiatives

School council members and parents need to keep informed on

sensitive political issues such as choice legislation. The home and school association is the first and most logical group with whom to begin this initiative, since two of the five purposes of the Catholic home and school association deal with information sharing.

Those purposes are: "to provide parents and teachers with the information to aid in all aspects of education and the students' growth and development" and "to organize political action of the parents as advocates regarding local, state and federal legislation that affect Catholic schools as well as the lives of students and parents."

Obvious means of communication are the school newsletter and the parish bulletin. News that is concise, accurate and current will have the greatest impact on keeping parents well informed. An update at each school council meeting is essential. Furthermore, interested parents could invite several friends to an evening tea for discussion on current issues.

The finance committee could dream about the impact of a law giving help to parents. How would the budget be affected and how would the school's long-range plan be altered?

Since most political action involves contacting legislators, a knowledge of the fundamentals of lobbying is essential. Beginning with the two points given below, the home and school association can research specific ways to put them into practice. (See the article "Political Action: The Practical Role of the Principal" on page 29.)

- Constituents should contact their own representatives as a legistator will always be more responsive to someone he/she represents.
- A well-prepared communication is personal, brief, factual, timely and specific.

Other creative ways of keeping parents and school council members informed involve the students, particularly junior high and high school students.

These students could prepare and stage a debate on choice legislation at the home and school meeting or during a local senior citizen program. A political update can be a part of the morning announcements.

Students may invite elected officials to have lunch in the school cafeteria or join them on the local radio or television talk show for a discussion about educational issues. A current news bulletin board in a prominent place in the main school corridor could include articles on proposed legislation.

As principals, we can further the work of the National Congress by communicating the story of the academic excellence and religious effectiveness of Catholic schools and by celebrating their success.

Moreover, we can ensure the future of these schools by informing and motivating parents and members of school boards to support school choice at federal, state and local levels.

Resources

Bridging Schools and Community, Pennsylvania School Boards Association, Inc., 1989.

Coons, John E. and Frank J. Monahan, *Political Action, Public Policy and Catholic Schools,* Washington, DC, NCEA, 1991.

Menicucci, David, *Catholic Home and School Association Guidebook,* Washington, DC, NCEA, 1990.

News release, "Catholic Educators Praise GI Bills for Children: Say Quality Education Is Civil Rights Issue for 90's," NCEA, June 25, 1992.

Valerie Grondin, OSF
St. Hedwig School
Toledo, Ohio

Section III
School
and Society

The Challenges of Living in a Global Society

The best gift that we can offer our school community is to respond to the call of the National Congress of Catholic Schools for the 21st Century. We are beginning to see a society where technological advances make it possible for all people to be closer. The future holds many exciting possibilities and many demands for today's students. Our challenge as educators is to prepare our students for a global society.

When we were in grade school, we were saving pennies to adopt "pagan babies." It wasn't important where they lived, their culture, the color of their skin—we were doing something for "the other side of the world." Today, our students go home to India for a visit, vacation in Italy or help to build houses in Mexico. There is no "other side of the world" for students today.

As the National Congress set priorities in November 1991, the following statement ranked sixth out of the 25 ratified: "We will educate students to meet the intellectual, social and ethical challenges of living in a technological and global society."

This challenge is not new. We have always professed to teach the total person to live to his/her potential in the world of today and the future. We have been working on this for years. But we are asked now to review our programs and perhaps refocus our efforts.

For the purpose of discussion, we will reflect on the intellectual, social and ethical challenges of living in a global society, and how we as principals can make a difference. We hope to stimulate thinking and energize action in the local school. We cannot do it alone; we need the involvement of all staff, parents and students in order to realize and integrate these elements.

Intellectual challenges

In educating students to meet the intellectual challenges of living in a global society, it is important that a principal:
- Be visionary

- Provide real experiences for teachers
- Develop programs that motivate, not teach everything

A visionary principal discerns the challenges and restructures curriculum and classrooms to meet those challenges. Sister Martha Rolley, speaking at the NCEA Principals Academy, told us that students in the classrooms of tomorrow need to be "players"—active learners with the ability to think technology. Our responsibility is to build active, creative, social and technology-rich learning environments for, as our world changes, so do our classrooms.

Educational research indicates that the teacher-centered classroom is no longer effective. Just telling students pages and pages of facts does not guarantee learning. Today's teacher must not be a "sage on stage," but a "guide on the side" in a learner-centered classroom where relationships are explored and quality of work is valued.

As we envision the changing role of teachers, we need to investigate methods of staff development and in-service that actively involve the teachers. James Banks provides an example when he says, " The most meaningful and effective way to prepare teachers to involve students in multicultural experiences that will enable them to know, to care, and participate in democratic action is to involve teachers themselves in multicultural experiences that focus on these goals."

In a global society, it also will be very important for principals to work with teachers to develop programs that motivate students to want to learn. These programs need to develop critical thinking and problem-solving skills so students will know how to learn. We can help teachers realize that the role of schools is not to teach students everything, but to produce independent life-long learners.

Social challenges

We would like to focus on two main challenges of living in the global society:
- Building better relationships with ourselves and others
- Living in our multicultural and multi-ethnic world

It is an accepted fact that a positive self-image enables us to get along with others in most situations. If we don't see ourselves as valuable, we cannot see the worth of anyone else. We teach "love your neighbor as yourself," often presuming that we do love ourselves.

One task of the school environment is to reinforce self-esteem so that students can function positively. Many people fail at their jobs not because they can't do the work, but because they cannot get along with other employees.

A staff must have a plan to promote self-esteem on a consistent basis. A few beginning-of-the-year activities will not ensure success. An ongoing process must be planned and integrated into our total curriculum. Teaching self-esteem is one of the most important things we do as educators.

Studies show that cooperative learning encourages acceptance by peers for handicapped and minority students, for gifted as well as at-risk and average. This interdependent learning style develops social skills and self-esteem.

School and Society topic discussions at the National Congress raised another social concern. Participants agreed on the need for multicultural programs and structures that are nonsexist, nonracist and nondiscriminatory. We need to incorporate into the curriculum the contributions of men and women of diverse cultures. Equally important is the need to recruit and hire staff that reflect a multi-ethnic, multiracial and multicultural society.

The second resolution of the Association for Supervision, Curriculum and Development (ASCD) for 1992 called for a multicultural education that is not the "melting pot" but a "mosaic" concept. "The mosaic image focuses on the whole, yet allows recognition of any part as important to the whole," reads the ASCD resolution. We will not effectively reach students if we give them the message that their culture is inferior and the "American way" is superior. This mosaic model helps us realize the need to recognize, value, utilize and celebrate cultural differences.

Ethical challenges

An interactive learning and teaching model of value education is needed to enable students and teachers to live in a value-oriented environment. Many issues demand our reflection and command a high priority in our curriculum. In fact, it is our response to these issues that allows us to be different. A few of these issues are:

- Family
- Women's rights
- Respect for life
- Special needs students
- Ecology
- Peace and justice

We are called to infuse and reinforce this missing link in education in our Catholic schools. But even more important is that our schools espouse gospel values.

Another area deserving comment is the media—radio, television and print. We are increasingly challenged to provide our students with objective responses to current situations. In fact, it is just as

61

challenging for us to separate fact from opinion. The 1992 Los Angeles riot and political campaigns are good examples of events that can be presented to students and families infused with our own values and philosophy.

We also call attention to the value of patriotism/freedom. Too often patriotism goes no further in the classroom than a salute to the flag. The concept "American" can be comforting and offers a secure feeling as we struggle with the realities of equality in our multi-ethnic society.

Without question, we stress the importance of drawing our ethnic parents into planning sessions which specifically deal with cultural issues, language implementation and programs that promote or highlight individual cultures. This investment can be rewarding in building total community.

We cannot shy away from these issues simply because they tend to be controversial. If we don't teach the values and importance of ethical decisions, who will? "Parents are at a loss because they themselves do not know what they believe and so have no self-confidence in telling their children," says Father Francis Kelly, former NCEA director of religious education. "So, they wish off that responsibility to the school."

Father Kelly reminds us to communicate to our students the scriptural moral principle enunciated so clearly by St. Paul (1 Cor 6:19): "You are not your own." We are children of God and live his message with each other.

Making a difference

The following practical suggestions are offered to principals who wish to address the ethical, social and intellectual challenges in our school communities.

Principal initiated

- Investigate the possibilities of a student exchange program with other countries. If possible, take a group of students to another country.

- Provide quality in-service to teachers, as well as time, compensation and ways to share regarding:
  —new technology
  —learning disabled
  —societal problems such as gangs, violence, drugs
  —other

- Hire teachers and staff of multicultural and multi-ethnic background if possible.

- Address current issues as they occur and are presented in the media. Offer alternative and appropriate responses to these events.

- Encourage teachers to get to know their students and their cultural gifts by:
  —knowing and using full name, spelling and pronunciation
  —making home visits to get to know the family and home environment

- Consult with parents and involve them in planning for multicultural curriculum, programs and events.

Staff development
- Discuss the discipline policy and how it is being enforced through the values of self-esteem, justice, peace and love.

- Find a way to teach social issues so they enhance the curriculum without frustrating the teacher. Some approaches are: Vision and Values, D.A.R.E., AIDS education, "World of Difference"

- Discuss cooperative learning and small group work as important learning tools in teaching children.

- Train staff in the use of technology. Look at the technology you already have and where you want to be in the future. Design a plan for technology use in your school.

- Encourage staff to agree among themselves to address any act of unkindness and give immediate feedback. Acts of kindness should also be recognized. This action crosses all grade levels.

- Make an annual plan for multicultural awareness and activities. It should be included and integrated in the total curriculum (social studies, art, music, language, games, etc.) along with special celebration points throughout the year.

Parental involvement
- Invite parents to share their talents and culture with the students:
  —during a regularly scheduled time each week
  —in "mini" classes of enrichment periodically

63

—as opportunities come up in the curriculum

- Provide parent seminars on various values and societal issues such as:
  —new technology
  —how to evaluate the impact of media on students
  —ethnic gifts and prejudice and how to live as "citizens of the world"

- Encourage families to have one night a week without T.V. so they can experience their own family culture and customs together.

- Invite parents of different ethnic background to plan a cultural celebration. Let parents decide the who, what, when and how. Some times might be:
  —Kwanza   —Martin Luther King, Jr.
  —Chinese New Year   —Cinco de Mayo
  —International Fair   —Culture Festivals

Student involvement
- Bring the world of cultures and diversity to the school by involving parents and the civic and parish community as a part of the experience.

- Urge students to attend with their family multicultural festivals and public celebrations held in your city.

- Identify with students the values they consider important. List these values and prioritize them. Use this information to understand the perspective the students bring to the class.

- Conduct "class meeting" to address a value issue when needed. Don't wait for the scheduled time.

- Formally teach students how to evaluate the media and its impact on us, our country and our value system.

Conclusion

We can no longer "adopt pagan babies" to teach global awareness. The challenge is to make our students aware of multicultural ethnicity, and to develop that awareness into understanding, acceptance and collaboration. An effective educational leader will take steps to meet the challenges.

But first we must educate ourselves for the future by accepting and understanding change. Only then can we influence our staff and parents as we partner with one another to educate our children for the 21st century.

Sister Catherine McNamee, NCEA president, says this so well:

> ...a school that can bring...classroom instruction, liturgical services, shared reflection on the gospel message, daily interaction with a community of students and teachers committed to Christian vision and values—only such a school can provide the total education that our children and youth deserve. This is the 'value-added' dimension our parents and students have every right to expect.

The challenge is ours! Let us respond and offer the gift of our leadership to the church and our nation!

Resources

Association for Supervision, Curriculum and Development, "Resolutions 1992."

Banks, James A., "Multicultural Literacy and Curriculum Reform," *Educational Horizons,* Spring 1991.

Borba, Michael, "Self-Esteem, Self-Value," *Today's Catholic Teacher*, February 1992.

U. S. Catholic Bishops, *Putting Children and Families First: A Challenge for our Church, Nation and World,* Washington, DC, U.S. Catholic Conference, November 1991.

Coughlin, Bernard J., "Who, Then, Will Teach Them?" *Inland Register,* November 19, 1987.

Everett, Katherine L., "Cooperation: Can It Deliver?" *Momentum*, April 1992.

Henry, George J., "Viewpoint on School and Society," *Momentum*, April 1992.

Kelly, Francis, "Who Is the Contemporary American Catholic?" *Momentum*, February 1988.

Guerra, Michael, Regina Haney and Robert J. Kealey, *National Congress on Catholic Schools for the 21st Century: Executive Summary,* Washington, DC, NCEA, 1992.

The Catholic School and Society, Washington, DC, NCEA, 1991.

O'Neil, John, "Tap Student Strengths," *Update*, ASCD, June 1992.

O'Neil, John, "A Generation Adrift," *Educational Leadership,* September 1991.

Ozar, Lorraine A., "Catalyst for Change,"*Momentum*, April 1992.

Pryor, Carolyn, "Sister Schools for Building International Relations for Children," *Phi Delta Kappan,* January 1992.

Stotsky, Sandra, "Academic vs. Ideological Multicultural Education in the Classroom," *The American School Board Journal,* October 1991.

Shanker, Albert, "The Pitfalls of Multicultural Education," *The International Educator*, April 1991.

Catherine Kamphaus, CSC
Our Lady of Lourdes School
Salt Lake City, Utah

Becky Piela
St. Mary Magdalene School
Columbus, Ohio

Carol A. Speltz
St. Mary's School
Spokane, Washington

Let There Be Peace

I give you a new commandment: love one another. As I have loved, so you should also love one another. This is how all will know that you are my disciples, if you have love for one another. (Jn 13: 34-35)

The American bishops' pastoral *To Teach As Jesus Did* (1972) presents to Catholic school principals three challenges:

- To teach all subjects well, and especially the Gospel of Jesus Christ
- To form community through which the presence of God is experienced in the midst of a faith-filled people
- To serve others after the example of Jesus

Any school that identifies itself as Catholic must endorse these three essential institutional qualities.

It is an understanding and acceptance of the second challenge—to form community—that affords the Catholic school principal the means and hope of moving from a climate of violence to a climate of peacemaking in the school. The Catholic school principal promotes this climate of peace by understanding and promoting the concepts of:

- Community formation
- Self-esteem
- Conflict management

Community formation

Understanding what it means to form community is to create a school climate that reproduces, as far as possible, the warm and caring

67

atmosphere of family life. If the quality of caring for every child is evident, then the school affirms that every child is important, a child of God who is "cared for when hurting and challenged when drifting—cared for and challenged ultimately because the members of the community, students as well as teachers and parents, are the body of Christ."

Church documents further describe the Catholic school community. From the first moment that a student sets foot in a Catholic school, he or she ought to have the impression of entering a new environment, one illumined by the light of faith, and having its own unique characteristics, "an atmosphere enlivened by the gospel spirit of love and freedom." (*Christian Education*, 8). This sense of community promotes a love that excludes no one. Students know their teachers; teachers know their students. A rapport is established simply by their talking to one another.

In such an environment the interpersonal relationships of its members are strengthened, based on love and Christian freedom. School goals are agreed upon by teachers, students and families alike, and an atmosphere of cooperation and collaboration exists in achieving those goals.

All members, as good stewards, are willing to accept responsibility, individually and corporately, for the way each lives, uses time, talent and treasure, and responds to the needs and rights of others. (*Sharing the Light of Faith*, 70) Human rights are, therefore, the minimum conditions for life in community. (*Economic Justice*, Preface, 17)

If this understanding of community is accepted, then the opportunities of its members to move from dealing with violence to fostering peacemaking are present. Their self-esteem is healthy and any conflicts that may arise can be addressed in the peaceful manner found in the early church:

> They devoted themselves to the teaching of the apostles and to the communal life, to the breaking of the bread and to the prayers....All who believed were together and had all things in common. (Acts 2: 42-44)

The Catholic school principal is acutely aware of the importance of building community. Opportunities are numerous. The following activites are just a few that foster community building with students:

- Teachers greeting each student upon arrival and/or dismissal
- Cooperative learning activities
- Celebrations of students' achievements
- Prayer, retreats, liturgies, paraliturgies
- Faculty/student activities, e.g., volleyball games
- Involving children in setting school goals through the student council and service activities

Building self-esteem

In the Gospel, Jesus urges us to love our neighbor as we love ourselves. Many of the students we greet each day need to learn to love and respect themselves before they can love and respect their neighbor. In former years, family structures enabled children to develop feelings of self-worth and provided communal experiences which nurtured the child's self-concept.

According to Thomas Lickona, today's supportive classroom community provides the surrogate family entity that meets the emotional needs of students. This theory is reiterated by the National Conference of Catholic Bishops ad hoc committee on the family, which notes that only 10% of American families now live in the "traditional" family arrangement of working father, stay-at-home mother and one or more children.

How can we, as Catholic educators, help raise children's self-esteem? The following ideas, while by no means exhaustive, offer some practical suggestions for administrators and educators.

Unity circle. The objective of the unity circle is to give participants a chance to speak in the presence of a group in which they know they are accepted. Each session of the unity circle begins and ends with prayer. At the beginning of the school year, each person in the circle shares one quality he/she likes about each member of the group. In this way, each child hears many positive things about him/herself. During subsequent unity circles, the children may share something about themselves and their families. Unity circles build a sense of trust and well-being among the class and provide the time and place for sharing among students and teacher.

Cooperative learning. Cooperative learning encourages students to work together rather than compete against one another. According to William Glasser, working as team members satisfies the need for belonging and the need for power. The team offers many opportunities for students to contribute to the group. Children who are part of cooperative learning teams develop a sense of worth as they learn to agree and disagree with each other in a peaceful manner.

Big brother, big sister. Within the school community, it is possible to pair off older students with younger students. The students interact in a variety of ways:
- Tutoring
- Reading to one another
- Accompaning each other to school liturgies and other school functions

69

Older students enjoy taking responsibility for the younger students; younger students enjoy the attention of older students. A sense of community develops within the school.

Rewards, awards. Children appreciate frequent positive strokes. Any type of verbal praise is appropriate, but youngsters also respond well to behavior modification charts and to monthly or quarterly award ceremonies where children receive certificates for academic and social achievements. In many geographic areas, businesses are willing to offer incentives for positive behavior and good attendance.

Goal setting. Age-appropriate and realistic goal setting will allow children to monitor their academic and social progress. Seeing progress in any given area enhances self-esteem.

Commercial programs. Several book companies presently offer ready-made programs which educators may adapt to their students' needs.

The National Congress on Catholic Schools for the 21st Century affirmed the belief that the Catholic school creates a supportive and challenging climate which affirms the dignity of all persons within the school community. By fostering each students' self-esteem, we bring this belief to reality.

Conflict management

The bishops' pastoral *The Challenge of Peace* urges all of us to work for peace. It is our responsibility to help our students take an active part in bringing peace to our schools, to their families, neighborhoods and, ultimately, to the world. This is not an optional commitment, but a requirement of our faith. We are called to be peacemakers, not by some movement of this time but by our Lord Jesus Christ.

Dealing with conflict is part of the work for peace. Violence has become very much a daily occurrence in the lives of our students. We must understand this if we are to teach our students the gospel value of nonviolence as an alternative to violence. Unfortunately, violence creates distrust and becomes an obstacle to building community.

Children need to be taught nondestructive ways to settle conflict in order to live in peace and harmony. Conflict management skills can be used by students throughout their lives. When students learn to handle conflict in a peaceful way, their self-esteem improves. They feel good about themselves and become more responsible for their actions and better able to handle future problems.

Research states that conflict management is the creative response to conflict in the context of a supportive, warm, caring community. The goal of conflict management is a peaceful community, an atmosphere which supports the growth of self-esteem and successful accomplishments.

Elizabeth Loescher writes about a successful conflict management process which teaches young people to resolve conflict in a constructive way. The process has six steps:
1. Identify and define the conflict
2. Generate all possible solutions (brainstorm)
3. Evaluate all ideas
4. Choose the best solution
5. Implement the solution
6. Reevaluate

Student mediation programs also have been widely and enthusiastically endorsed by educators around the country. Where the programs have been used, educators see a marked improvement in the lives of the students in the schools. In schools where mediation is provided, students are encouraged to bring their problems to a trained peer mediator who helps them to set common goals, explore alternatives and agree on a solution to the problem.

In setting up a peer-mediation program, the following steps are suggested:
1. Select/hire a consultant who trains some of the teachers and students in conflict resolution
2. Select some of these students for further training as mediators
3. Educate all the students about peer mediation
4. Design referral forms, permission slips and consent agreement forms
5. Select a mediation site
6. Use all means of communication to help spread the idea of mediation as an alternative to violence

If we are to affirm the dignity of our students and reduce the violence in our schools, we have no choice but to provide opportunities for students to creatively and cooperatively work together in peace.

Resources

Borba, Michele and Craig, *Self Esteem: A Classroom Affair,* Harper San Francisco, 1978.

Brandt, Ron, "On Students' Needs and Team Learning: A Conversation

71

with William Glasser," *Educational Leadership,* March 1988.

Convey, John, *The Catholic School and Society,* Washington, DC, NCEA, 1992.

Guerra, Michael, Regina Haney and Robert J. Kealey, *National Congress on Catholic Schools for the 21st Century: Executive Summary,* Washington, DC, NCEA, 1992.

Heft, James and Carleen Reck, *The Catholic Identity of Catholic Schools,* Washington, DC, NCEA, 1992.

Heister, John W., Director, Cooperative Resolution of Conflict, New York, 1992.

Kreidler, W., *Creative Conflict Resolution*, Glenview, IL, Scott, Foresman Company, 1984.

Lickona, Thomas, "Four Strategies for Fostering Character Development in Children," *Phi Delta Kappan,* February 1988.

Loescher, E., *Conflict Management: A Curriculum for Peacemaking,* Denver, CO, Cornerstone: A Center for Justice and Peace, 1983.

Lynch, Thomas, "What Is the Method in Today's Family Madness," *Momentum*, September 1987.

Prutzman, P. et al, *Friendly Classroom for a Small Planet,* Philadelphia, PA, New Society Publications, 1984.

U.S. Bishops, *The Challenge of Peace: God's Promise and Our Response,* Washington, DC, U.S. Catholic Conference, 1983.

Paul E. DeZarn
St. Raphael School
Louisville, Kentucky

Ann Christi Brink, CSJ
St. Anthony of Padua Neighborhood School
Syracuse, New York

Lorraine Burns, SSND
Holy Family School
Rochester, New York

We Are Called to the Table: A Look at Diversity

All activities of the human species are in a constant state of evolution. We are, in fact, a life force on this planet that will continue to evolve in a journey of change and maturation. Individuals learn first to crawl, then walk, and some even grow into long-distance runners.

We must concentrate on the journey. We must determine, from the very beginning, the destination we hope to reach. This destination may change, or become the future launch site for a new venture. Regardless, we must know where we want to go, and the paths we wish to take.

This basic premise is true for all life's undertakings. Nowhere is it more evident than when we speak of multiculturalism in America. Where do we, as a nation, want to be when we enter the next millennium? How do we intend to get there? Where are we now?

I invite the reader to reflect with me for a few moments by opening his/her sensory receptors with the gift of imagination.

Reflect upon the one experience common to all of us—eating. I love Mexican and Italian food. I love German and Mideastern food. I love Irish stew and...well, you get the picture. Actually, I have been told that there is no plate I would pass up, and I guess, at 245 lbs., there may be some truth to that.

The basic nourishment provided by the food we digest, and the joy it offers us as it passes over our taste buds is a common experience. Some people need to know all the ingredients that go into the food they consume, along with understanding how it was prepared. This is of no importance to others. There are those who cannot digest certain foods or spices.

But no one wants to be force fed. No one wants to be told what to eat day after day. It is actually unhealthy to eat the same food day after day, whether it be sauerkraut or tacos. Variety is not only the spice of life, it is the sustenance of life.

Regardless of the type of food placed before us, we should be able to appreciate and honor the work that goes into the many varieties of nourishment produced by the human family. They are, after all, part of the celebration of the banquet of the Lord.

How then do we prepare ourselves and our students for the festive celebration of multiculturalism?

Let us first begin to crawl.

First steps

When we formulate the calendar for our school year, we can select a day for a multicultural fair. The Sunday during Catholic Schools Week would be a good choice. At the beginning of the academic year this event can be pointed out to the staff with the expectation that all be present and participative. This may be the "open house" for the school, an experience offering insight into the pluralistic world in which we live.

The journey to this goal must be plotted out and prepared for. Committees, those beasts of burden that travel so slowly but carry so much weight, must be developed. This very important step develops ownership within the community.

Food committee. A group of parents or the parents club might form this committee. Their task would be to organize a group of volunteers to prepare a variety of different ethnic foods to be served during the open house. A small sign by each plate explains the dish. Parents may dress in appropriate costumes and provide a variety of music from different countries as background.

Liturgy committee. A group of parents and teachers may plan the main Sunday liturgy to take place just before the open house. The theme of celebrating differences can be tied into Catholic education and the liturgy can incorporate elements of various world cultures. Stated and explained in the bulletin, these may include African attire for the celebrant, wine from Italy, water from France.

Display committee. A group of teachers can organize individual student and staff displays for public viewing. The works might include visual presentations of an individual's family tree or national background, as well as oral stories from the family history or culture. Pictures, drawings or artifacts could be displayed.

Projects committee. A group of parents could seek out entertainment groups representing different cultures, both from the school community and from the larger community. These performances could take place during the open house, or at different times during the week leading up to the event.

Walking our walk

As our multicultural plan gets moving, a number of projects can enrich our understanding of and appreciation for the variety in our human family. The suggestions below may be incorporated into the open house event or developed as learning experiences in themselves.

T.V. reviews. Students will enjoy being assigned to watch television for the evening. Their task would be to write down the time of each program, the title, the different nationalities portrayed, and the ways in which they are depicted. The nightly news is an important program for this project. Even the commercials should be detailed.

The students should then imagine that they are extraterrestrials who are visiting the planet and have only T.V. from which to make judgments about our world. They should write a short report to their leader explaining the different types of people they saw, their reflections on those people, and the reasons for those reflections.

Family speakers. Parents and grandparents could be invited to share with the students the stories of their backgrounds, and the history they have lived through. They could talk about their jobs and even their dreams for the future.

Student test. The students may be asked to make up a test that looks into different cultures. Four or five cultures would be chosen and items such as food, music, musical instruments, works of art, clothing, celebrations or geographical locations are matched to the appropriate culture.

The celebration of the uniqueness of the many different people who populate this planet is extremely important. It should be a constant consideration as we plan in-services, select textbooks, develop prayer services and hire staff. A variety of functions and formats are important.

However, more daring and costly steps also need to be taken. The crawling and walking is done.

Long-distance runners

Peter Senge in the book *The Fifth Discipline* writes: "Organizations learn only through individuals who learn. Individual learning does

75

not guarantee organizational learning. But without it no organizational learning occurs....Taking a stand for the full development of your people is a radical departure from the traditional contact between employees and institution."

We must start to budget real dollars toward the growth of our teachers in multicultural understanding. Conventions such as the one offered by the National Catholic Educational Association, along with instructional experiences offered by multicultural organizations are mind-expanding events that help teachers understand other people and their views. The opportunity to meet with colleagues from different parts of the country and the world broadens teachers' perspectives and, in turn, the perspectives of their students.

Are we willing to invest the money in our staff to allow them to go to various locations in the world that call out in a special way for the attention and understanding of our church? Will a teacher or principal give witness to the pain of Soweto, South Africa? What impact will the poverty of Arcato, El Salvador, have on someone who instructs our youth? Time spent in the crime-infested ghetto areas of our country or in the underdeveloped Native American reservations allow a teacher to bring the truths of others to our youth more accurately.

What about a student and staff exchange with schools in other parts of the globe? Can we exchange with Russia, Jordan or Japan? Can we afford to? Can we afford not to?

Above all else, we must have a vision for the future. Without a vision, we will never complete the journey.

The Japanese concept known as "Kaizen" is helpful as we approach this issue. In his book *Kaizen*, Masaaki Imai argues for the importance of constant improvement, a gradual and never-ending process. Continued attention and constant evaluation must be invested in our plan.

We must challenge ourselves to walk forward. The penalty for complacency is far more severe than the mere halt of progress: regression, even atrophy occurs. The human family cannot risk this, especially in the area of understanding and acceptance of one another.

Finally, I challenge the reader to reflect upon the American culture. It does exist. It may be young in comparison to many world cultures, but it has evolved over hundreds of years. It celebrates the richness of diversity, based upon the concepts of freedom, perserverence and God-given rights. Our credo calls us to reach out to all, especially those who are in need.

Arthur M. Schlesinger, in his book *The Disuniting of America*, expresses the need for Americans to concentrate on our common humanity. He argues the importance of emphasizing that which brings us together rather than that which separates us.

We must never lose sight of our oneness by excluding others. This is not our way. It is not the way of Christ. After all, "We are Sons of the morning. We are Daughters of day. The one who has loved us has brightened our way. The Lord of all kindness has called us to be a light for His people—to set them all free. Let us build the City of God. May our tears be turned into dancing, for the Lord, our Light and our Life, has turned the night into day."

Resources

Imai, Masaaki, *Kaizen: The Key to Japan's Competitive Success,* New York, Random House, 1986.

Schlesinger, Arthur M., *Disuniting of America: Reflections of a Multicultural Society,* Knoxville, TN, Whittle Communications, 1991.

Senge, Peter, *Fifth Discipline: Mastering the Five Practices of the Learning Organization,* New York, Doubleday, 1990.

George Hofbauer
St. Joseph School
Seattle, Washington

Responding to Minority Students in Catholic Schools

Research indicates that 23% of children enrolled in our nations' Catholic schools are minority students. The recruitment of teachers representative of those minorities is a major challenge facing our principals, especially in inner-city schools.

Difficult enough is the task of hiring teachers who are dedicated and willing to sacrifice financially by teaching in a Catholic school. Nevertheless, the recruitment of minority teachers to be role models for these students must be a crucial consideration in the hiring process.

Catholic educators are obligated to embrace Christ's command to "Go and teach all nations." The selection of minority teachers and the training of our majority staff must be reflective of this gospel command. We must reach beyond our own cultural boundaries and enthusiastically embrace various ethnic backgrounds and cultures in our schools and communities.

Both minority teachers and minority-competent teachers in Catholic schools can enhance a true gospel education by ministering to our minority students. We can reach out with a Christ-like love and caring to these students who need to feel a part of our school families. These children can come to know and love Christ in a more affective way as we offer ourselves as true instruments and vehicles by which Christ's love can be felt.

To be true to our vocation and mission to provide a total education to all students entrusted to our care, every teacher must be a sensitive and prepared professional, competent in the multicultural, multi-ethnic and multiracial diversity of our nation and world. Our schools must not only reflect a deep understanding and appreciation of, but also celebrate this diversity.

This will require that supplemental studies of various cultures be added to our curriculum. Research and study of various religions, political structures, traditions and customs must be a part of our school. These ethnic studies can assist our students to study events from different perspectives, foster intergroup understanding, and instill an awareness and appreciation of various peoples and cultures.

Minority students excel in academics, self-concept and social acceptance where their culture and traditions are understood, accepted, studied and celebrated. Majority students also benefit from this type of education, as it broadens their appreciation of various peoples, fosters a deep understanding of peoples, reduces prejudice and fear, and fosters the wholistic education of a global community.

Implementing the following ideas into our school traditions will further our multicultural education goals:

- School liturgies and prayers can be centered around an ethnic theme, using cultural prayers, decorations, music.
- American Indian, European, Afro-American, Asian and other cultural studies will be deepened as students prepare reports, term papers, essays and other projects.
- Nationality Week can be celebrated by having students dress in native costume, present reports and share a meal of ethnic foods.
- Literature, poetry, stories and folklore of various cultures can be incorporated into language arts.
- Social studies programs are enhanced through comprehensive studies of various global cultures, capturing historical events from various perspectives and focusing on the cultural aspects of historical figures and their contributions to society.
- Representatives from various religions may be invited to present the fundamentals and traditions of their faith.
- Student and faculty exchange programs may be implemented.
- Correspondence programs with students from other countries can be fostered. This might include seeking information, literature and other materials from embassy officials.

These and other programs can help educate and inform our teachers, parents and students of the many unique and rich cultural traditions of minority groups within our community.

Historically, Catholic education has made great efforts to reach out to the minority children in our communities. This was evidenced by the European religious communities which came to this country to educate the immigrant children of their homelands. The great successes of these early Catholic schools came about because educators responded to the needs of these people.

We should secure this successful tradition in our schools today by recruiting teachers with great knowledge of and sensitivity and dedication to the minority students in our schools. Only then can we fulfill the command of Christ to "Go and teach all nations."

Resources

Educational Leadership, vol. 49, no. 4, December 1991.

Hall, Suzanne, ed., *Integral Education: A Response to the Hispanic Presence*, Washington, DC, NCEA, 1987.

James A. Banks, "Education For Freedom," *Focus In Change,* Summer 1992.

National Conference of Catholic Bishops, *To Teach As Jesus Did,* Washington, DC, U.S. Catholic Conference, 1972.

Phi Delta Kappan, January 1992.

Richard Martinez
Our Lady of Las Vegas School
Las Vegas, Nevada

Shaping a Multicultural People

Appropriately, a multiplicity of concepts surface when it comes to multicultural education. One school of thought firmly believes in the common culture, yet a diversity of opinions exist even among these educators. Fundamentally, advocates of the common culture stress teaching American history from the viewpoint of what Americans have in common so that a sense of national identity is developed.

Diane Ravitch, for instance, appreciates the contributions of all peoples who have come to our shores and says that "the common culture is not an Anglo-Saxon melting pot: it is an amalgam of the contributions of different groups that have joined American society and enriched our shared culture."

Others emphasize ethnocentricity, based on the teaching of individual cultures, and insist that children must be culturally centered and empowered in the classroom setting.

Ethnocentric adherent Molefi K. Asante, who believes that "one of the principal aspects of empowerment is respect," finds that "students are empowered when information is presented in such a way that they can walk out of the classroom feeling that they are part of the information."

Whatever the approach, the driving force in this decade is the need to pluralize the curriculum. Asa G. Hilliard gets to the heart of the problem when he says: "Ultimately, if the curriculum is centered in truth, it will be pluralistic."

Catholic school principals are the educational leaders in their schools and they must take a stand regarding multicultural education. How can they lead and what should be the focus of their attention? Yes, they believe in multicultural education, but on what basis shall they exert their leadership toward this end?

83

One answer gives us focus and direction—Christ the leader said, "I am the way, the truth, and the life." Our philosophy as Catholic educators is Christocentric.

Presenting the vision

Principals can create the climate to effect change in our Catholic schools when they are centered in Christ and firmly convinced that truth must prevail. Although a variety of avenues are used to achieve the goals of Catholic education, the guiding principle is the education of the whole person who will grow into the likeness of Christ and be filled with the gifts of the Holy Spirit.

During periods of long-range planning, principals and their staffs collaborate as a team to establish realistic goals. During this time principals share the vision which they feel impelled to put into action in order to effect change. Because of the many facets involved in executing such a vision, principals must provide time for reflection and discussion, especially with those who will be directly involved.

At the outset, some goals related to multicultural education can be proposed with the intention of revising them to meet the specific needs of the school. Some suggestions are:
- To strive to continuously strengthen the faith community among the faculty, staff and school board through a planned program
- To work toward an increased awareness and acceptance among parents of all people in a diversified society
- To formulate a realistic curriculum balancing both American history and multicultural studies

Specific objectives to meet these goals are necessary. The role of the principal is to share the dream with the teachers and to delegate to them some responsibility for shaping this dream. If there is "ownership" of the mission, the vision and the dream, the outcome will certainly be successful.

A few suggested objectives to carry out the proposed goals are:
- To allow time to form a faith community through prayer, retreats and social activities with faculty, staff and school board
- To delegate to parents, through the home and school association, the opportunity to plan educational and social programs on multicultural education and to establish a better understanding of different peoples
- To focus on multiculturalism in staff development and curriculum planning

84

Designing the program

Whatever action principals take, they need to be guided by the makeup of the school community. Each program will be different depending on the nature of each situation.

If a school is racially mixed, the program must meet the needs of all students. If it is predominantly made up of one race or cultural group, the needs will naturally be different. Whatever the situation, principals will be challenged to initiate a program taking into consideration the variety of cultures of their student population.

In an article in *Educational Leadership,* three teachers—Bonnie Sue Adams, Winifred E. Pardo and Nancy Schniedewind—clearly state the challenge for all educators:

> Our challenge as educators is first to help ourselves and our students become conscious of our culture—to be able to step outside of ourselves and look at the habitual norms, values, practices that make up our culture—and to appreciate it. The second task is to see that "our way of doing things" is not the only, or the right way and to understand that others have their ways. Such cultural consciousness helps us to value our culture without seeing it as normative, and to respect a variety of cultural experiences.

The challenge for these teachers in a school district in Long Island, NY, was that their school, predominantly white, middle class and Christian, had "prevailing practices [which] reinforce majority group experience." They met this challenge by attempting to "effect staff and student attitudes, curriculum materials, awareness of cultural diversity, and power relationship so that those personal beliefs and institutional characteristics that have systematically denied some children equal opportunity can be changed."

This school system adopted the Human Rights Education Program. Catholic schools could do likewise, building on the fundamental basis that Catholic education must be Christocentric. The three focus areas of the Human Rights Education Program are:
1. Education for diversity and social responsibility
2. Cooperative learning and cooperative educational practices
3. Conflict management/resolution and peace education

Devising a plan

In planning multicultural studies, four major groups should be kept in mind: Native Americans, Afro-Americans, Hispanics and Asian-Americans. Three disciplines can share the responsibility for a multicultural studies program: religion, social studies and language arts.

Grades one through four could take a general approach, emphasizing education for diversity and social responsibility. With an interdisciplinary approach in grades five through eight, ample time would be available for a unit in multicultural studies, possibly accommodating the current course of studies used in the Catholic school.

For example, in American history, taught in both fifth and eighth grades, the Native American experience could be studied in the fifth grade and the Asian-American experience in the sixth grade. The Afro-American culture could be the focus in the seventh grade and Hispanic peoples in the eighth grade.

Regardless of the approach, a multicultural curriculum is essential in Catholic schools today. Cultural understanding requires a great deal of time and effort on everyone's part. Catholic schools, with their Christocentric focus, can challenge their entire educational community to recognize, appreciate and work together to become a multicultural people.

Resources

Adams, B.S., W.E. Pardo and N. Schiendewind, "Changing the Way Things Are Done Around Here," *Educational Leadership,* December 1991, pp. 37-42.

Asante, K.A., "Afrocentric Curriculum," *Educational Leadership,* December 1991, pp. 28-31.

Hilliard, A. G., "Why We Must Pluralize the Curriculum," *Educational Leadership,* December 1991, pp. 12-14.

Ravitch, D., "A Culture in Common," *Educational Leadership,* December 1991, pp. 8-11.

Today's Catholic Teacher, March 1992.

Dawn Gear, GNSH
St. John Neumann Regional Catholic School
Liburn, Georgia

Multicultural Approaches in the Catholic School

At the National Congress on Catholic Schools for the 21st Century, John J. Convey of The Catholic University of America outlined 10 challenges facing Catholic schools if they are to ensure their continued viability.

Convey believes that a commitment should be made to increase access to Catholic schools for "special populations," i.e., racial and ethnic minorities, and to make provisions for financial assistance to these students if needed.

The second part of his challenge is of equal or greater importance: that Catholic schools which serve special populations develop programs that acknowledge and reflect the culture, values and traditions of these populations.

This challenge would place Catholic schools in the stream of a recent movement in education which insists on inclusion of "underrepresented populations"—mainly racial and ethnic minorities, women and the handicapped—in the curriculum and teaching. The current term to describe this movement is multicultural education.

Catholic schools' traditions, environment and curricula are already imbued with the gospel values of acceptance, respect and appreciation of others. Nevertheless, the following specific objectives should be added:

- To provide students with a sense of their ethnic and cultural heritage
- To provide students of each ethnic group with information about the unique cultures of other ethnic groups

Schools using a multicultural approach recognize that children come to them with traditions, beliefs and practices already developed through membership in a particular family, neighborhood or cultural group. Multicultural education emphasizes the ways in which each culture addresses basic human beliefs, needs and desires. The sense of heritage, identity and pride of each culture can stimulate not only curiosity but also understanding and acceptance. This knowledge and these experiences are the beginning of appropriate instructional experiences.

Incorporating and acknowledging the contributions of men and women of diverse cultures and races in the curricula needs to be addressed by everyone on the staff. The principal or curriculum director needs to provide an in-service opportunity aimed at an understanding of the importance of these contributions and, whenever possible, for writing a curriculum for this subject area.

Other ways to incorporate cultural diversity include the following considerations.

Textbook selection. When selecting textbooks, check to be certain that they include many cultures and races. Do reading texts present a variety of stories about men and women from different cultures and races? Do social studies texts provide unbiased and objective information on different cultures and races and highlight persons from these groups who have made significant contributions to society? Do music textbooks present songs of different traditions and languages, including sign language? See the Appendix for a checklist in selecting textbooks.

Art. The styles and techniques of different cultures and races, as well as particular artists representing these groups and, if possible, samples of their work should be a part of the curriculum.

Religion. Particular religious customs and traditions can be taught and incorporated into paraliturgies and liturgies. The lives of the saints from many different cultures offer opportunities for research and reflection on diversity.

Multicultural week. During this week each class or student can come dressed in a particular culture's native dress. Persons can be invited from the different cultures and races, both to speak and to entertain, i.e., dances, music. A food fair is an excellent way to see and taste a variety of ethnic foods. Multicultural achievements in the arts and sciences may also be part of this special week. Parents can be invited to attend some activities.

Involvement with another school. Interaction with a neighboring school whose student body is enriched with a variety of cultures is a great way to reach beyond one's own boundaries. This can be done through a pen pal program or a sharing of activities. Another way to reach beyond one's school is to have a student exchange with children from different regions of the U.S. or other countries.

Library reading. By monitoring the students' library reading and SSR (sustained silent reading) time, teachers can ensure that students are becoming familiar with the stories of men and women from different cultures and races.

Calendar clues. Particular days set aside to honor different cultures and races, such as Native American Day, St. Lucia, Martin Luther King Day, Presidents Day, Hanukkah and Cinco de Mayo, offer opportunities for celebration and study.

The curricula can acknowledge and incorporate the contributions of men and women of diverse cultures and races in many ways. Through readings and brainstorming with other faculty members, educators can generate a variety of ideas.

Resources

Convey, John J., "Catholic Schools in a Changing Society," *The Catholic School and Society,* Washington, DC, NCEA, 1992.

"History Texts Cover the Sideshows, but Often Miss the Main Event," *Curriculum Review,* April 1990, pp. 5-6.

Norton, Donna E., "Teaching Multicultural Literature in the Reading Curriculum," *The Reading Teacher,* vol. 44, no. 1, pp. 28-40.

"Peace Corps Volunteers Launch Pen Pal Program," *Curriculum Review,* May 1990, p. 14.

Appendix
Checklist for Choosing Multicultural Instructional Materials

1. Are the five approaches to multicultural education addressed?
___race/ethnicity
___social class
___language
___gender
___handicaps

2. Is the material written by historians, authors or consultants representative of the above groups?

Barbara O'Block
Our Lady of Knock School
Calumet City, Illinois

Carol Seidl, OSF
Immaculate Conception School
Yuma, Arizona

The Principal and Multicultural Staff Development

Multicultural staff development in Catholic schools? How does this fit into our mission? A distinguishing mark of a Catholic school is the presence of a faith atmosphere in which students and teachers alike discover and nurture the image of God in one another. If this atmosphere of discovery and nurturing is to be a reality, it needs to be addressed within the context of all cultures present in the community.

The National Congress on Catholic Schools for the 21st Century provides a starting point. At this congress a number of directional statements were developed for Catholic schools including this pointed declaration regarding minority presence in the Catholic school: "We [Catholic schools] will aggressively recruit, retain and develop staff to reflect the needs of an increasingly multiracial and multicultural society."

Catholic schools are typically identified as high achieving schools, where students excel in reading, math and science. A significant intervening variable that may impact this achievement level is the growing multicultural population in Catholic schools. The percentage of minority students in the schools has increased from 10.8% to 23% since the 1970-71 school year.

This developing situation provides principals with a challenge that needs to be aggressively addressed. If we are to maintain our level of academic success with all students, this growing population cannot be ignored or underserved.

The reality

The growing diversity among our student population calls for a diverse focus to our curricular strategies. An inclusive strategy is needed that will not separate or isolate, but rather celebrate and appreciate our many cultures and their unique perspectives.

Multicultural education, as opposed to assimilationist education, is a process whereby cultural behavior and cultural differences are regarded as teaching and learning tools used to create a fair system that ensures all students an equal chance to acquire social, academic and personal skills. It is not limited to the study of ethnicity and is not viewed only as a concern for minorities, according to Jack Kehoe.

It is imperative that our entire population gain greater understanding and empathy for the cultures that create our whole. "A fundamental goal of Catholic educational institutions is to provide quality education and equal opportunity," note the authors of *A Catholic Response to the Asian Presence*. "In spite of this altruistic purpose, however, many ethnic groups have suffered as a result of the assimilationist philosophy which equates equality with a systematic absorption into the dominate culture."

The challenge then is to create a situation where the development of true community replaces this domination with a multicultural perspective.

The direction

James Brooks, a professor of education and director of the Center for Multicultural Education at the University of Washington, Seattle, says that the goal of multicultural education is an education for freedom through developing skills:

- To participate in a free society
- To participate freely in other cultures and groups
- To participate in social and civic activies to make a situation more free

Anne Turnbaugh Lockwood notes that Brooks identifies research showing that interventions supporting these goals of multicultural education can have a lasting impact if they are implemented early in the school experience.

If interventions are to take place, they will depend upon the efforts of the teachers. In order for principals to facilitate the necessary changes, Brooks says that they will need to understand their own ethnic and cultural history. Only then will they be able to understand and "connect" to other cultures.

It should be obvious that the achievement of a multicultural effort will rest on the substance and success of the staff development program. Teachers can't give (or support) what they don't have!

Principals, along with the faculty/staff, need to identify the challenge of the multicultural situation in their school and proceed to develop a plan to address local priorities.

Staff development models are common in the educational literature. Insights regarding possibilities are explored by the Association for Supervision and Curriculum Development (ASCD) in its 1990 yearbook, *Changing School Culture Through Staff Development.* Options are proposed for staff development that call for the teachers to increase their flexibility in meeting change by becoming life-long learners. In addition to addressing typical constructs for content and technical skills, reflection on teacher activities is proposed.

Through reflecting on learner and practitioner activities, the teacher has a greater possibility of internalizing these activities and becoming a perpetual learner, one who is constantly moving toward improvement and understanding. This is critical in the area of multicultural development.

Models

Given the wide variety of faculties and staffs in Catholic schools, no one clear and definitive model can solve the challenge of multicultural staff development for every school. A variety of approaches is possible. The important factor is that the challenge be addressed. Some processes that could be utilized as models for this type of staff development are suggested below. One doesn't need to reinvent the wheel. Just use it!

Mentoring. This approach to staff development is individual and personal. It provides a forum where persons from divergent cultures provide each other with a new perspective on a culture through personal interaction. A key component to this model, according to Mildred Haipt, "is that the participants proceed through it as peers in learning and personal growth."

Research in-service. Knowledge is the basis for understanding. Through an in-service on how and where to attain information on other cultures, or even one's own culture, a base line understanding can be developed as a catalyst for further development and understanding, says Ewa Pytowska, writing in *Momentum.*

Practioner resources. These resources are supportive of many of the other models, but are often such significant sources of information that they need to be mentioned on their own merit. Examples of resources published by NCEA include: *Integral Education: A Response to the Hispanic Presence; A Catholic Response to the Asian Presence; The People: Reflections of Native Peoples on the Catholic Experience in North America.* The information and insight these books provide

93

are invaluable.

The programmatic approach. An aggressive and long-term approach to multicultural staff development may adhere to a specific model or program. Typically, these programs are funded through government or private grant monies that will provide ongoing training and support.

One example of this type of program is the Intercultural Training Resource Center in the Archdiocese of Boston, described by Pytowska. To support the instructional aspects of this program, a key element is its focus on the creativity of teachers to support their research and training.

SEED (Seeking Educational Equity and Diversity) is another example of a funded program. As described by Cathy Nelson, a distinguishing aspect of SEED is its focus on the vehicle of inclusive curriculum in the school to promote multicultural understanding.

Based on the articulated belief that Catholic schools are commited to educating students of diverse backgrounds, provisions need to be activated to realize this commitment and maintain it. Options are available to us. We need to start, perhaps simply, but we need to start!

References

A Catholic Response to the Asian Presence, Washington, DC, NCEA, 1990.

Catholic Elementary and Secondary Schools 1991-92, Annual Statistical Report on Schools, Washington, DC, NCEA, 1992.

Catholic Schools for the 21st Century: Executive Summary, Washington, DC, NCEA, 1992.

Changing School Culture Through Staff Development, ASCD Yearbook, 1990.

Haipt, Mildred, "A Guide for the Voyage," *Momentum*, November 1990.

Integral Education: A Response to the Hispanic Presence, Washington, DC, NCEA, 1987.

Kehoe, Jack, "Enhancing the Multicultural Climate of the School," *History and Social Studies Teacher*, vol. 9, no. 2, December 1983.

Lockwood, Anne Turnbaugh, "Education for Freedom," *Focus in Change*, The National Center for Effective Schools Research & Development, Summer 1992.

Nelson, Cathy L., "The National Seed Project," *Educational Leader-*

ship, January 1992.

Pytowska, Ewa, "The Teacher as Cultural Researcher," *Momentum,* November 1990.

The People: Reflections of Native Peoples on the Catholic Experience in North America, Washington, DC, NCEA, 1992.

James T. Brennan
Holy Spirit School
Fremont, California

Section IV
Educational Technology

Tech-Know-Alice: Survival in Wonderland

"I'm late! I'm late!" yells the White Rabbit.

Alice of Wonderland fame runs after him questioning, "For what?"

But White Rabbit disappears. Alice chases him, but he's nowhere to be seen. In his place is a strange caterpillar who promptly asks, "Who are you?"

Alice's reply is simple, "I am Alice!"

"But, who are you?"

"I guess I'm just a Tech-No-Alice! I have no survival skills for this wonderland! Who's going to give them to me so I can successfully contribute to society in this 21st century?"

"The Mad Hatters (educational leaders) of the Catholic schools will see to that, my dear," chime in Tweedle-Dee and Tweedle-Dum.

"Beware the Jabberwoch!" a voice admonishes.

"But I don't know what that is!" responds Alice.

"That, my dear, is the technocrat, who thinks only of technology and not about you as a person," answers the Mock Turtle. "Our society is video-based and visually oriented, say our educational researchers and our partners in business. Therefore, Alice, you'll just have to boot up and down-link with the times.

"You need not worry, Alice. The Mad Hatters are becoming increasingly attuned to the concept that a portion of their mission as Catholic educators is to make learning as exciting and as interesting as the MTV you watch every day. Classroom technology (including networked computers, quality educational courseware and multimedia tools) has even more pizzazz than television.

"You will become an active learner, and teachers will become what they have always been meant to be—facilitators of learning.

"As managers of the educational process, teachers find themselves free to do more individualized instruction, to teach creatively, to motivate, to inspire and to meet total educational needs. You will see yourself transformed into 'Tech-Know-Alice'," concludes Mock Turtle.

The Mad Hatter survival kit

With great dignity, the Mad Hatter challenges, "Our task as educators is to prepare Alice for the world of tomorrow, my fellow Mad Hatters, a world in which technology gains momentum and is expected to double each week. Alice must be prepared for a world of information overload. Let's give her survival skills to cope in this wonderland of the 21st century.

"**Comfort with technology** is the survival skill Alice must learn first. As educational leaders, we must call on every financial resource at our disposal to bring before Alice the varied technological wonders available in her wonderland. Make sure your tea party staff knows that you support them not only by being a cheerleader for technology, but also by modeling the use of technology yourself.

"**Communication skills** are a necessity if Tech-Know-Alice is to survive. Look closely at your language arts curriculum. Is too much time being spent on the written word and keyboarding skills? Alice will be using computers without keyboards in the 21st century. Alice's ability to communicate verbally will greatly impact her use of technology. Now look again, closely, at your language arts curriculum. As an effective educational leader, you will see to it that Alice has command of the verbal skills equal to, if not better than, the written word.

"**Flexibility** is a must for an educational leader. Alice will thank you for giving her flexibility as a survival skill in wonderland. She will face a rapidly changing job market. Empower her with the basics (which Catholic schools do very successfully) and give her the ability to accept change.

"**Life-long learning skills** must be embraced by Alice. Her teachers, under your direction, will be facilitators. They will encourage Alice to work well with others as well as on her own. Tech-Know-Alice must become a life-long independent learner, but wonderland also will insist that Alice collaborate with her peers to be successful.

"**The ability to analyse** the technology explosion will be Alice's because you, as Mad Hatters, choose curriculum materials that reinforce critical thinking skills. You see to it that the teachers receive workshop training. Then, as classroom facilitators, they can give Alice the 'freedom' to use critical analysis and problem-solving skills when dealing with situations in her daily life."

The Queen of Hearts for the arts

"No! No! No! Stop! I can't stand all this talk of technology!" shouts the Queen of Hearts. "Where are those finer things? You know, those things that are the essence of civilization? The arts!" Her highness punctuated her words by throwing her croquet mallet at the King of Hearts.

"Of course Alice needs experiences in dance, theater, speech, music and visual art. You can't expect her to sit at a computer all day! She's gotta feel...she's gotta express...she's gotta create.

"All this technology will leave her a cold, mechanical robot unless you allow her the time and space to express her softer, more human side. After all, Tech-Know-Alice has a soul and her spiritual self needs to be given wings to soar.

"I propose that ensuring survival of the arts includes:

- Designing curriculum goals for Alice that will incorporate the arts, i.e., expressive language, movement/dance, music, visual arts, storytelling, drama and creative writing
- Writing performance objectives for each area of Alice's art curriculum
- In-servicing Alice's teachers to integrate art experiences throughout the curriculum
- Enlisting Alice's parents to share their special talents by providing art opportunities
- Utilizing arts and humanities groups, museums, theater and music groups, and artists in Alice's school
- Incorporating aesthetic experiences such as viewing and listening to live performances
- Giving Alice opportunities every year to exhibit and perform
- Teaching Alice to be media literate by:
  — logging her time spent listening to and/or viewing various media
  — having her identify forms of media
  — enabling her to critically analyse those forms for stereotyping, propaganda techniques, values

"It is through the arts that Alice's feelings and insights can emerge in a world gone mad with technology in the 21st century. So, let's find a place where Alice will be more than just one of many in the deck of cards, where she will be nurtured and her gifts encouraged.

"Or off with your heads!"

Tea party impacts

"Well! Let me tell you," chant Tweedle-Dee and Tweedle-Dum in unison, "in a classroom with networked computers, teachers can challenge Alice by giving individualized assignments while monitoring her successes from work stations. This individualization may help to head off learning problems she may encounter before remediation is needed. The emphasis will shift from imparting data to Alice as a passive listener toward discussion, analysis and synthesis of ideas where she will cooperatively share in the learning process.

"Alice's class has some fast learners, some slow learners and countless learners somewhere inbetween. In a classroom enriched with technology, Alice and her friends can progress at a pace limited only by their ability. No risk of embarrassment, judgment or criticism.

"Because Alice will be learning 'what matters' in her daily life, her self-confidence and self-esteem will be enhanced. Technology will give Alice a feeling of 'can do.'

"Her self-esteem will also improve because Alice will be able to manage a lot of her own learning.

"Yes, little Alice can make choices in a risk-free environment where, regardless of her ability level, she will learn real-world problem solving and critical-thinking skills within a flexible environment which has access to resources beyond her classroom or the school building."

"Well, Tweedle-Dee and Tweedle-Dum are a little pompous, but they do make some sense," interjects the Queen. "Perhaps their heads won't have to roll after all!"

"It seems to me," drawls the Caterpillar, "this interrelation of technology and the arts makes education more than learning to cope, it makes it learning to lead!"

"I'm late! I'm late for the 21st century!" exclaims the White Rabbit as he grabs Alice and pulls her up through the rabbit hole. "All of the characters that you have met in this wonderland of technology are seeing to it that you are prepared."

"Oh, thank you! Thank you! At last I can be Tech-Know-Alice!"

Resources

Braun, Ludwig, "The Worth of a Child," *Momentum*, February 1992, pp. 10-13.

Brigham, Frederick H., Jr., "The New Astronauts," *Momentum*, February 1992, pp. 8-9.

Dede, Christopher, "The Evolution of Information Technology: Implications for Curriculum," *Educational Leadership,* September 1989, pp. 23-26.

Eisner, Elliot W., "The Misunderstood Role of the Arts in Human Development," *Kappan*, April 1992, pp. 591-95.

Godfrey, Robert, "Civilization, Education, and the Visual Arts: A Personal Manifesto," *Kappan*, April 1992, pp. 596-600.

Hurley, Kathleen M., "Integrating Technology into the School," *Today's Catholic Teacher,* November/December 1990, p. 12.

IBM, "Technology and the Classroom of the 1990's," Supplement to *Today's Catholic Teacher*, October 1990.

IBM, "Technology Today for Your Catholic School," Supplement to *Today's Catholic Teacher,* October 1991.

Rolley, Martha, "Computers in Administration and in the Classrooms," National Catholic Principals' Academy, July 1992.

Zukowski, Angela Ann, "Technology Beyond the Computer," National Catholic Principals' Academy, July 1992.

Michael A. Casper
St. Vincent de Paul School
Fort Wayne, Indiana

Barbara Mathe
St. Benedict School
Cambridge, Ohio

Helen Stanford Smith
Monte Cassino School
Tulsa, Oklahoma

Technology for Instructional Purposes: Ready—Set—Go!

Technology is changing rapidly and the development of new technology takes place daily. These developments include not only computers, but also telecommunications, desk-top publishing, satellite transmissions and media. This technology affects our classrooms and students, our parents and publics.

Just as principals in Catholic schools are widely diverse, so are the programs now in place with regard to technological development. How can we, as principals, make a positive difference in the new revolution sweeping through education?

Getting teachers ready

Daniel Kinnaman states in the October 1990 issue of *Technology and Learning* that "good administrators are like gold...supportive, provide opportunities for their staff to be involved and are willing to allow teachers to leap four walls in a single bound." In order for principals to prepare their teachers for technology, we propose the "3 R's" of staff development in this area:

- **Release time:** substitute teachers, creative scheduling, redistribution of nonteaching responsibilities
- **Remuneration:** stipends, continuing education units, graduate credit
- **Recognition**: staff trainers, local and/or diocesan presenters, local and/or diocesan publicity, participation in technological teams at local or diocesan levels

One major role of the principal as instructional leader in creating a vision for the educational use of technology is to seek out in-service programs which will help the teachers carry out the established plan of action.

105

Setting the stage

A second major role is that of facilitator of curriculum programming. The technological curriculum is inclusive throughout the classroom setting, in addition to a computer lab setting. Curriculum planning is established by each individual school, based on goals and needs.

As we face the 21st century, technology and telecommunications bring the world into the classroom and the home. Therefore, the curriculum plan, which recognizes this important fact, is supported, even pioneered by the principal.

Technology challenges today's educators to design imaginative lessons to inspire young minds to explore, to discover, to learn. In today's "learning center"—be it the living room, classroom, library or parish hall—students can master much more than facts or fundamentals. Listed below are the skills students need for the future:

- To organize resources
- To work with others
- To acquire, evaluate and use information
- To understand complex work systems
- To work with a variety of technologies

It seems appropriate at this stage in education not only to use "learning communities" rather than just one classroom and one school, but also to strive for global awareness. Our learning communities, then, will extend beyond our own cities, states and nations. This will be accomplished by:

- Pen pals via satellite
- Lessons via video discs
- Foreign languages via closed-circuit television
- Specialized individual school plans via student imagination

We need the vision to see the direction and speed of society's changes and to be proactive, not reactive. The audacity to change the very culture of our schools, and to broaden how we teach, is a challenge we all face.

Go for it

Our third major role is to provide the materials and/or monies necessary to accomplish this move to a technological education. Every school situation is different, and the needs are different. Therefore, the principal, in consultation with the entire staff, should investigate the following areas for funding:

- Corporations
- Government programs (federal and/or state)
- Business partnerships/donations

- Foundation grants
- Lease purchase agreements
- Vendor contributions
- Parent-teacher organizations
- Individual sponsors
- Alumni programs

Once the necessary materials have been acquired, the principal's role continues. Assuring the coordination and application of technology in sync with the goals of the school program is vital. The link between the teachers, curriculum and materials is centralized around the principal. The changing structure of schools calls for a new system of leadership which is circular. Leaders are no longer at the top but in the center, connected to those around them—reaching out.

Just as our teachers are using technology creatively to excite students about learning and to increase their capacity to understand all academic subjects, we as principals are exciting our teachers about technology. We are enhancing their capacity to understand the direction technology is taking, not only in their future but, more important, in the future of students.

The students are ready—the teachers are getting set—now the principals must go!

Resources

Kinnaman, Daniel E., "Staff Development: How to Build Your Winning Team," *Technology and Learning*, October 1990.

National Congress on Catholic Schools for the 21st Century: Catholic School Governance and Finance, Washington, DC, NCEA, June 1991.

Ristau, Karen M., "The Challenge: To Provide Leadership Within Catholic Schools," *National Congress of Catholic Schools for the 21st Century—An Overview,* Washington, DC, NCEA, June 1991.

Rolley, Martha, "Computers in Administration and in the Classroom," National Principal's Academy, July 1992.

"Technology or the Teacher—or Both," *Momentum*, February 1992.

Wilson, Tom, "Where to Find Funding for Your Technology Project," *Technology and Learning,* January 1992.

Zukowski, Angela Ann, "TTN: A New Network for Technology-Oriented Teachers," *Momentum*, September 1991.

Linda L. Cherry
Saint Mary School
Delaware, Ohio

Joel Miller, MSC
Holy Family School
Port Allen, Louisianna

The Tool Kit of Technology

It is time to move past the question of whether or not technology is worthwhile in schools. The time is ripe to focus on the more important questions: What is the best mix of technological capabilities? What are the conditions under which these capabilities can be used effectively with various student populations and in different learning environments to meet a wide variety of educational goals?

Preparing students

Educators can turn to a growing tool kit of technology applications for help as they prepare students to lead and prosper in an information-based society. Change is the only constant in today's workplace—and communications and problem solving are replacing manual skills.

Technology can help prepare students to find their way through change. The tool kit of technology looks beyond the standard computer use to highly interactive ways students can learn subject matter and, at the same time, gain powerful access to extensive information.

A look at multimedia

Multimedia technology is the educational buzzword of the 90s. Among the many definitions of multimedia, perhaps the most common is that given by Tom Greaves, manager of K-12 Educational Technology for IBM: "Multimedia is the use of sound, still images, animation, motion video, text and graphics in a single computer application."

Tom Wilson, director of Technology for the Corona-Norco Unified School District in Corona, California, states, "The key advantage of multimedia is the multisensory appeal. Learning theories say students learn best when they hear, see, write, are actively involved in learning—which suggests that multimedia can help teachers reach all students."

Some of these technologies are already being applied in schools, while others are hovering on the horizon. Principals should build a technology glossary; the following terms will provide a start.

Telecommunications. Combining a telephone line, an inexpensive modem, free or inexpensive telecommunications software, and even the simplest of computers opens a vast world of on-line communications to schools. With telecommunications, schools have access to extensive data bases of information, instructional activities and personal communications with thousands of other educators and students, overcoming barriers of distance and time.

Classrooms can become windows on the world as they connect with experts and other classrooms around the globe. This technological experience has a profound impact on students' knowledge of world cultures and helps to prepare them for life-long learning in a world where telecommunications will be a primary source of information.

Compact Disc Interactive (CD-I). They look like music CDs, but CD-Is can display pictures, videos, graphics, sound and text with which users can interact.

Compact Disc-Read Only Memory (CD-ROM). Like CD-Is, these disks hold massive amounts of information, but they are not interactive.

Digital Video Interactive (DVI). This new technology can compress and then decompress video at a rate of 30 frames per second. They will let teachers and students have access to text, full-motion, full-color video and audio in a choice of languages.

Optical Fiber. Fiber-optic technology allows multimedia to be put in motion on an information highway of vast potential. Fiber-optic cable has many advantages over the traditional copper cable. It carries more information, maintains a stronger signal strength, is not subject to magnetic interference that could otherwise disturb signal quality, requires less space, and has a longer life span.

Video Microscopy. Video microscopy lets science teachers use a microscope as a tool for group instruction. This system depends on a color video camera, a large screen monitor, a small control monitor, stereoscopic and compound microscopes, an electronic pointer and a fiber-optic light of variable intensity.

With video microscopy, teachers can demonstrate techniques and analyses of microscopic research on screen. Teamed with a video cassette recorder, the system can provide lessons for later use as well as for live instruction.

Two-way Satellite. Students in some areas of the United States have been using satellites to take long-distance instructional courses for years. With a two-way satellite system, students can now ask questions of the instructor and he/she can see the students. A fax machine allows teachers and students to send written materials to each other.

On-Line Cable Services. Via cable, schools can receive a variety of information. Also, many local cable companies allow schools to use their studio and their equipment to produce school-related programs.

Liquid Crystal Display (LCD). An LCD allows the projection of a computer image onto a large screen using an overhead. A cord from the LCD plugs into one of the ports on the back of a computer. The LCD is placed directly onto an overhead projector, similar to a transparency, allowing the teacher to use the computer in whole-class instruction.

Close-Captioned Learning. Close-captioned television is a technology that schools could use not only to serve the needs of the hearing impaired, but also to help English-as-a-Second-Language students improve their skills.

Laptop Computers. Pencils, slide rules and calculators became standard classroom equipment over the years. Laptop computers for each student may well be standard equipment in the classrooms of the future.

Interactive Videodisc. Each side of disc can hold up to 54,000 images, including movies and stereo sound. With special software, students can splice together different images from the videodisc to create their own presentation.

Direct Broadcast Satellite (DBS). This high-powered transmission system promises to expand vastly the availability of video, software data and communications abilities in schools. DBS equipment is a mere 1.5 feet in diameter (much larger satellite dishes are used today) and hopefully will be inexpensive.

Networking. The linking of computers to transfer or share data.

Microcomputer Based Laborary (MBL). A sensory probe that can measure temperature, light, sound or motion, an MBL plugs into the back of a microcomputer and transforms it into a sophisticated laboratory.

Integrated Learning Systems. Software for basic skills drill, tutorial, testing and evaluation have been around for a number of years. These systems are now incorporating on-line encyclopedias, word processors, calculators and graphing tools.

New visions of reality

The existing and merging electronic media—in all their shapes, forms and modes of transmissions—are giving students access to more lifelike and comprehensive visions of reality. This technology is suggesting new and exciting strategies to improve the ways teachers teach and students learn.

The challenge is to integrate technology into the curriculum to transform schools into active, vital work and learning environments. Here students can seek information from a variety of sources around the world, critically evaluating and integrating this information and collaborating with fellow students to solve problems.

Resources

Greaves, Tom, "Multimedia: What Is It? Where Is It Going? How Do You Begin?" *Today's Catholic Teacher,* October 1991, pp. MM4-MM5.

Grunwald, Peter, "Telecommunications in the Classroom," *The Executive Educator,* October 1991, pp. A4-A11.

Mageau, Therese, "The Decade of Technology," *Instructor*, January 1991, pp. 116.

Mageau, Therese, "The Real World Catalyst," *Agenda*, Fall 1991, pp. 54-57.

Wilson, Tom, "Here's What's New on the School Technology Horizon," *The Executive Educator*, October 1991, pp. A11-A13.

Cheri Gardner
St. John the Baptist School
Savage, Minnesota

Instructional Technology Is Now

Education today is the process of training students for the 21st century as we shift from an industrial to an informational era. If principals believe that statement is true, they can no longer be satisfied with the status quo. Teaching methods throughout our buildings should include a variety of technological applications.

Before a school can begin to use technology for instructional purposes, administrators and teachers must sit down and chart the course, asking themselves:
- Where do we want to go?
- How can our curriculum be enhanced using technology?
- How can the administrator use technology?

Where do we want to go?

The market today is flooded with all sorts of technological equipment and software. To avoid the purchase of large amounts of unrelated technology, a master plan must be developed. The classroom/lab use of technology is a part of the plan, not something that a teacher uses as a filler for a lesson.

Since the teacher is a mentor and guide for her/his students, principals should see that their staffs are properly trained in the use of instructional technology and are aware of technology that may be available in their community, such as satellite dishes, radio stations and cable television stations.

How can our curriculums be enhanced?

In the past computer labs were used for instruction of students by special computer teachers. Computer instruction was an isolated subject with no real connection to the total curriculum. While this concept was good for the time, these designated computer teachers

113

are now seen as **technology coordinators** and the labs function as research centers using computerized encyclopedias.

The real action is taking place in the classrooms, where teachers are using computers not for drill or reenforcement but for **introducing new concepts** or as a **stepping stone for discussion.** These computers can be linked to videodiscs or modems. Using interactive equipment, a wide variety of technology can be used to develop one concept, thus respecting students' **different learning styles.**

Elementary schools interested in introducing **foreign languages** but stymied by a limited budget might find it helpful to use cable television or an interactive computer program for this purpose.

Cooperative learning is a current favorite in education. What better way to work with this model than to have students work in groups using various forms of technology?

Audio conferencing can provide students with opportunities to meet the authors of books, or to be introduced to new ideas, concepts and cultural developments by specialists in various fields. This is especially enjoyable for elementary age students. The specialist can engage their curiosity and make subject matter come alive for them.

Computers are helpful for **less able learners.** In the area of creative writing, for instance, they find it much more meaningful to correct their work on the computer rather than having to rewrite it. They find the computer most helpful when doing any kind of written work. Chapter 1 programs in some areas are using computers for the instruction of these students, offering them opportunities to develop their basic skills.

Library services have greatly improved with the computerization of card cataloges and encyclopedias, giving students ready access to these materials. Librarians are also able to keep on top of overdue library books and to check quickly on circulation.

The **effective use of teachers' time** also enhances the curriculum and aids student learning. The cry of teachers today is that there is so much paper work to do and so many student papers to correct. When teachers use the computer to assist them with their work, this time can be greatly reduced, allowing more interaction with individual students.

How can the administrator use technology?

As the instructional leaders of their schools, principals clearly need to make efficient use of their time as well. Principals should design a **communication plan** for their offices. All class lists, schedules, textbook inventories, reports and memos can be done on the computer. Once these materials are in the computer, hours of work will be saved each year. Fax machines give the principal a quick way of communicating, as does electronic mail.

Many of the dioceses throughout the United States have had their schools join a program called **CONNECT.** This allows the diocesan school office, quickly and efficiently, to communicate with member schools, and allows the schools to have access to the news that comes across the wires. Various other segments are also available on this system. Principals can in-service their teachers through this use of telecommunications, enabling their professional staff an opportunity to interact with other professionals.

Principals also may wish to explore the use of **cable television** and **video cameras** as a means of making announcements throughout the school. This technology can also be used for teacher and parent training. The video camera is useful in preparing lessons for students who are absent from school for a long period of time and need to keep abreast of their studies.

I have shown how some of the current technology can be used to enhance the curriculum and to assist the administrator. Since technology is changing so rapidly, some of these suggestions may become obsolete. Thus the importance of interactive equipment. New ideas in technology will not stop. Principals need to begin their adventure into the technological world now.

Resources
Braum, Ludwig, "The Worth of a Child," *Momentum*, February 1992, pp. 10-14.

Kinnaman, David, "Strategic Planning for a New Generation of American Schools," *Technology and Learning,* September 1991, pp. 20-30.

Trotter, Andrew, "Technology in Classrooms: That's Edutainment," *The Education Digest,* January 1992, pp. 3-7.

Donna Marie O'Brien, OP
Saint John the Apostle School
Clark/Linden, New Jersey